USDA

United States
Department
of Agriculture

Forest Service

Northern
Research
Station

General Technical
Report NRS-6

April 2007

Slow the Spread: A National Program to Manage the Gypsy Moth

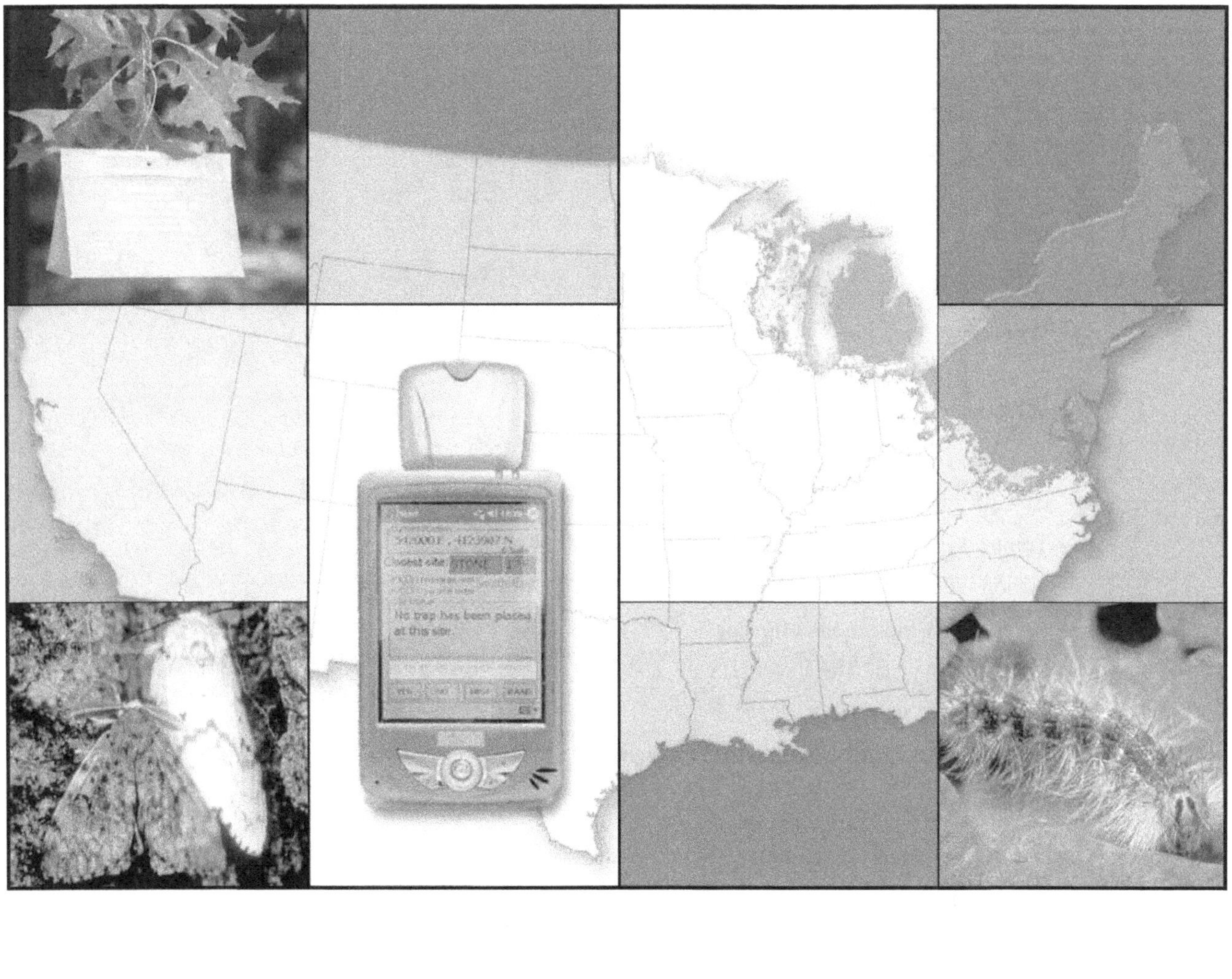

Abstract

The gypsy moth is a destructive, nonindigenous pest of forest, shade, and fruit trees that was introduced into the United States in 1869, and is currently established throughout the Northeast and upper Midwest. The Slow the Spread Program is a regional integrated pest management strategy that aims to minimize the rate of gypsy moth spread into uninfested areas. The premise of the Slow the Spread Program is to deploy extensive grids of pheromone-baited traps (>100,000 traps per year) along the expanding population front to identify and subsequently eradicate newly establishing populations to prevent them from growing, coalescing, and contributing to the progression of the population front. This report provides a brief history of the gypsy moth in North America, describes the dynamics of gypsy moth spread, and then details the technological and operational aspects of implementing the Slow the Spread Program.

Manuscript received for publication 25 October 2006

Cover:

(A) Delta trap. Terry Price, Georgia Forestry Commission (www.forestryimages.org).

(B) Male (Left) and Female (Right) Gypsy moth. John H. Ghent, USDA Forest Service (www.forestryimages.org).

(C) Trapper Gadget GPS-based "smart" data collection unit used in Slow the Spread for monitoring gypsy moth populations.

(D) Gypsy moth larva. USDA APHIS PPQ Archives (www.forestryimages.org).

(E) 2005 gypsy moth distribution in the United States.

Cover design by Laura Blackburn (USDA Forest Service, Northern Research Station)

USDA

United States
Department
of Agriculture

Forest Service

Northern
Research
Station

General Technical
Report NRS-6

April 2007

Slow the Spread:
A National Program to
Manage the Gypsy Moth

U.S. Department of Agriculture, Forest Service

Northern Research Station

11 Campus Blvd, Suite 200

Newtown Square, PA 19073

www.nrs.fs.fed.us

Tobin, Patrick C.; Blackburn, Laura M., eds. 2007. **Slow the Spread: a national program to manage the gypsy moth.** Gen. Tech. Rep. NRS-6. Newtown Square, PA: U.S. Department of Agriculture, Forest Service, Northern Research Station. 109 p.

The gypsy moth is a destructive, nonindigenous pest of forest, shade, and fruit trees that was introduced into the United States in 1869, and is currently established throughout the Northeast and upper Midwest. The Slow the Spread Program is a regional integrated pest management strategy that aims to minimize the rate of gypsy moth spread into uninfested areas. The premise of the Slow the Spread Program is to deploy extensive grids of pheromone-baited traps (>100,000 traps per year) along the expanding population front to identify and subsequently eradicate newly establishing populations to prevent them from growing, coalescing, and contributing to the progression of the population front. This report provides a brief history of the gypsy moth in North America, describes the dynamics of gypsy moth spread, and then details the technological and operational aspects of implementing the Slow the Spread Program.

Key Words: *Lymantria dispar*, biological invasions, integrated pest management, nonindigenous species.

Acknowledgments

We thank Paul E. Blom (Washington State University), Casey W. Hoy and F. William Ravlin (Ohio State University), Michael Connor and Richard C. Reardon (USDA Forest Service, State and Private Forestry), Kurt W. Gottschalk, Andrew M. Liebhold, and R. Talbot Trotter III, and Robert C. Venette (USDA Forest Service, Northern Research Station), and Kevin W. Thorpe (USDA Agricultural Research Service) for their helpful and constructive comments in preparation of this report. We also thank Martin J. Jones and Rhonda Cobourn (Production Services Team, USDA Forest Service, Northern Research Station) for their efforts in preparing this report for publication.

The development of the Slow the Spread Program would never have been possible without the efforts of countless individuals during the various pre-Slow the Spread stages, most notably William Dickerson (North Carolina Department of Agriculture and Consumer Services, retired), Victor C. Mastro (USDA Animal and Plant Health Inspection Service), José Negrón (USDA Forest Service), F. William Ravlin (Ohio State University), Richard C. Reardon (USDA Forest Service), and Robert Wolf (USDA Forest Service, retired). Also, Alexei A. Sharov (National Institute of Health) deserves special recognition for the development of the Decision Algorithm currently used in the Slow the Spread Program.

We are very appreciative of the efforts of Steven Crisp (Michigan State University), and Denise Dodd, Mannin Dodd, Shahrooz Feizabadi, Geoff Preston, and Jiang Wu (Virginia Polytechnic Institute and State University) who maintain an innovative information technology aspect for the Slow the Spread Program.

The very basis of the Slow the Spread Program would not be possible without the incredible efforts of our state partners, most notably Michael Massey and Steve Schmidt (North Carolina Department of Agriculture and Consumer Services), Larry Bradfield and Pat Somerville (Virginia Department of Agriculture and Consumer Protection), Clark Haynes and Matt Blackwood (West Virginia Department of Agriculture), Carl Harper (University of Kentucky), Brian Burke (Ohio Department of Agriculture), Phil Marshall and Zach Smith (Indiana Department of Natural Resources), Jim Cavanaugh and Nancy Williams (Illinois Department of Agriculture), Chris Lettau and Nick Clemens (Wisconsin Department of Agriculture, Trade and Consumer Protection), and Kimberly Thielen Cremers and Erich Borchardt (Minnesota Department of Agriculture). We also acknowledge the tremendous guidance and support of the Slow the Spread Operations and Technical Committees.

We also acknowledge the efforts of current and former state representatives to the Slow the Spread Foundation: Dave Adkins (Ohio Department of Agriculture), Charles

Kaufman (West Virginia Department of Agriculture, retired), Esther Chapman (Wisconsin Department of Agriculture, Trade and Consumer Protection, retired), Gene Cross (North Carolina Department of Agriculture and Consumer Services), Scott Frank (Illinois Department of Agriculture), Geir Friisoe (Minnesota Department of Agriculture), Frank Fulgham (Virginia Department of Agriculture and Consumer Protection), Gary Gibson (West Virginia Department of Agriculture), John Obrycki (University of Kentucky), Ken Rauscher (Michigan Department of Agriculture), Melody Walker (Wisconsin Department of Agriculture, Trade and Consumer Protection), and Bob Waltz (Indiana Department of Natural Resources).

Slow the Spread: A National Program to Manage the Gypsy Moth

Patrick C. Tobin, Editor and Contributing Author
Research Ecologist, USDA Forest Service, Northern Research Station, Morgantown, WV

Laura M. Blackburn, Editor
GIS/Statistical Assistant, USDA Forest Service, Northern Research Station, Morgantown, WV

Contributing Authors

Donna S. Leonard, Slow the Spread Program Manager, USDA Forest Service, Forest Health Protection, Asheville, NC

Andrew M. Liebhold, Research Entomologist, USDA Forest Service, Northern Research Station, Morgantown, WV

Michael L. McManus, Emeritus Scientist, USDA Forest Service, Northern Research Station, Hamden, CT

E. Anderson Roberts, Senior Research Associate, Department of Entomology, Virginia Polytechnic Institute and State University, Blacksburg, VA

Alexei A. Sharov, Research Scientist, National Institute on Aging/National Institutes of Health, Annapolis, MD

Kevin W. Thorpe, Research Entomologist, USDA Agricultural Research Service, Beltsville, MD

Amos H. Ziegler, Research Scientist, Department of Entomology, Michigan State University, Lansing, MI

Contents

Preface

Management programs for the gypsy moth in the United States comprise three components: 1) detection and eradication, 2) suppression, and 3) transition-zone management. Detection and consequent eradication of the gypsy moth occur in areas far from the expanding population front. This component is spearheaded by the USDA Animal Plant Health and Inspection Service in cooperation with state and local governments. In detection and eradication, pheromone-baited traps are used to detect the initial establishment of new populations in areas uninfested with gypsy moth; these areas can then be targeted aggressively. For example, there have been notable eradication efforts in Oregon and Missouri over the years. Gypsy moth populations that arise in the detection and eradication areas are largely the result of the anthropogenic transportation of life stages from areas infested with gypsy moth to those in which the insect is absent.

The suppression of gypsy moth populations is a management tactic used in the area that is generally infested, i.e., endemic. In this area, populations are known to exist but are not managed for the most part. In certain cases, such as the occurrence of widespread outbreaks particularly in residential areas and high-value timber stands where pronounced impacts may be expected, suppression tactics are used to limit the damage from high-density populations. This is a joint effort among the USDA Forest Service, state and local governments, and landowners.

Transition zone or barrier zone management, the third component of gypsy moth management in the United States, is designed to limit the spread of the gypsy moth specifically in a transition zone between the uninfested area (managed through detection and eradication) and generally infested areas (managed through suppression). This effort is conducted through the Slow the Spread (STS) Program.

This report addresses the STS Program from a technical perspective. A brief history of the gypsy moth in the United States is included in Chapter 1. This is followed by a review of the population biology of gypsy moth in Chapter 2. Chapter 3 addresses how gypsy moth populations are monitored under STS using innovative geospatial tools. Chapters 4 and 5 cover the computer-based Decision Algorithm that is used in the project to analyze trap catch data, identify isolated gypsy moth infestations, make recommendations, and evaluate the project's effectiveness. Chapter 6 focuses on data management and the web-based information delivery that is critical to the project. Chapter 7 covers the overall organizational structure, including the Slow the Spread Foundation, an innovative approach to implementing gypsy moth management over a large regional scale that involves multiple states and agencies.

Chapter 1. In the Beginning: Gypsy Moth in the United States

Michael L. McManus[1]

Early History

In 1869, egg clusters of the gypsy moth, *Lymantria dispar* (L.), were brought from France to Medford, Massachusetts (Fig. 1.1) by French lithographer Etienne Léopold Trouvelot (1827-95), who also was an amateur entomologist. It is believed he was conducting laboratory experiments to evaluate the gypsy moth as an alternative to the native silkworm, *Antheraea polyphemus* (Cramer). At that time, the European silk industry was severely affected by a protozoan disease, *Nosema bombycis* (Howard

Figure 1.1.—*Gypsy moth egg masses were intentionally brought to the United States by Etienne Trouvelot. However, life stages of the insect accidentally escaped from his home in Medford, Massachusetts (Trouvelot photo courtesy of the Mary Lea Shane Archives of the Lick Observatory, University of California, Santa Cruz).*

[1] USDA Forest Service, Northern Research Station, 51 Mill Pond Road, Hamden, CT 06514.

1930). There are various reports as to how the gypsy moth escaped from Trouvelot's home (Forbush and Fernald 1896); however, the ramifications of his actions referred to by some as an act of poor judgment and by others as a colossal blunder saddled North America with one of its worst pest problems (Liebhold et al. 1989). Since 1924, more than 34 million hectares have been defoliated by the gypsy moth (Fig. 1.2).

Once freed from the confines of Trouvelot's laboratory, gypsy moth larvae became established on vegetation in the immediate area. The infestation increased slowly and apparently was first noticed by local residents about 10 years later (Liebhold and Tobin 2006); however, they assumed that the gypsy moth caterpillar was native. It was not until the summer of 1889, 20 years after its introduction, that the gypsy moth became so abundant and destructive on fruit and shade trees that it attracted public attention. The extensive defoliation and nuisance created by enormous numbers of larvae were vividly described in Forbush and Fernald (1896).

The situation became so serious that on March 14, 1890, the State of Massachusetts appropriated $25,000 and delegated to the State Department of Agriculture the task of exterminating the pest. At that time, the infestation covered about 2,539 km^2 and encompassed 30 cities and towns in the greater Boston area. Control efforts were so successful that by 1899 there was little defoliation and relatively few moths were detected in residential areas. Nevertheless, 2 years earlier, Fernald, an entomologist with the Massachusetts Agricultural Experiment Station, estimated that eradicating the gypsy moth would require as many as 15 years at a cost of more than $1.5 million (Dunlap 1980). In February 1900, the legislature ordered the work discontinued because of the belief that the gypsy moth had been reduced to a minor pest (Perry 1955, Dunlap 1980).

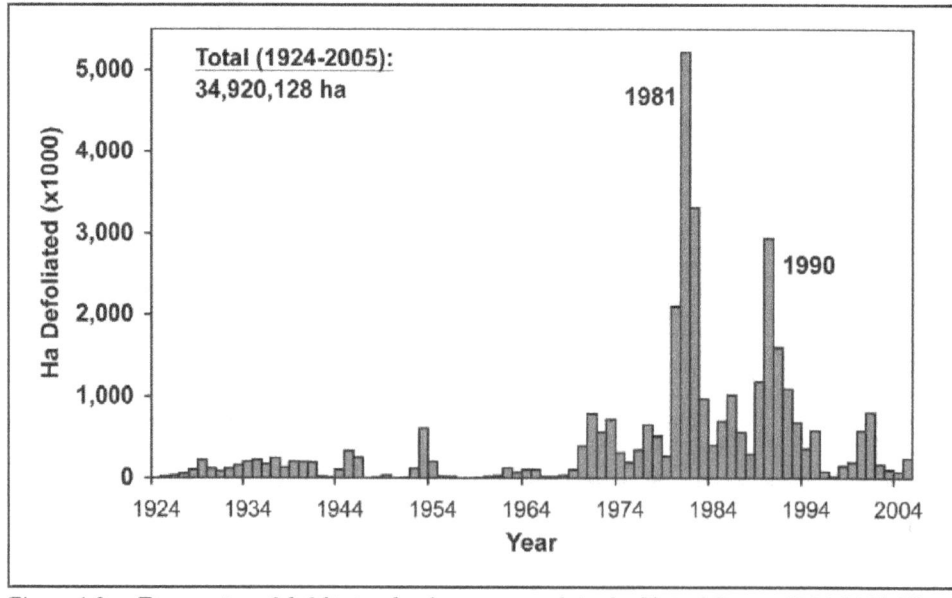

Figure 1.2.—*Time series of defoliation by the gypsy moth in the United States, 1924-2005. The most notable gypsy moth outbreaks occurred in 1981 and 1990.*

During the next 5 years, populations of the insect increased dramatically in the old infested area, and thousands of hectares were defoliated. Massachusetts resumed control work in 1905 and over the next 25 years spent more than $25 million on gypsy moth suppression (Dunlap 1980). By now, the infestation had spread to Maine, New Hampshire, and Rhode Island. In 1906, Congress appropriated money for the U.S. Department of Agriculture (USDA) to prevent the spread of the insect as egg masses and other life stages were being carried on commodities along major roadways. This led to the enactment of a domestic Federal quarantine against the gypsy moth in 1912 (Weber 1930).

Use of Barrier Zones Against Gypsy Moth

Despite efforts by the Federal and state governments, the gypsy moth continued to spread at an estimated rate of 10 km per year (Liebhold et al. 1992). By 1922, colonies were scattered farther west along the Vermont, Connecticut, and New York borders (Burgess 1930, Perry 1955, Dunlap 1980). Several isolated infestations also were discovered in states far from the generally infested area. In 1920, a severe infestation was found in Somerville, New Jersey, in a large stand of blue spruce trees that had been imported from the Netherlands in 1911 (Perry 1955, Davidson et al. 2001). This infestation, which covered more than 1,000 km^2 at the time it was discovered, was finally eradicated in 1931. Federal and state officials responded to this serious threat by establishing a Barrier Zone in 1923 that encompassed more than 27,300 km^2 and extended from Canada to Long Island along the Champlain and Hudson River Valleys (Burgess 1930) (Fig. 1.3). The territory east of this zone was treated by the individual states while infestations within the zone were eliminated by joint state and Federal actions. The Barrier Zone became generally infested by 1939 and suppression efforts were terminated in 1941 when funding was drastically reduced in part because resources were redirected to support the Nation's involvement in World War II.

It is noteworthy that the Barrier Zone was credited with effectively deterring the rate of spread of the gypsy moth for 16 years (Liebhold et al. 1992) even though only labor-intensive methods for control were available during that period and little effort was exerted in the rough terrain west of the Connecticut River. Felt (1942) prepared a position paper that strongly endorsed the renewal of efforts and funds to maintain the Barrier Zone and projected that if the gypsy moth were allowed to spread unimpeded throughout the range of white oak, defoliation on forested lands might reach 100,000 km^2 annually.

Gypsy moth populations expanded greatly during the early 1950's, at which time state and Federal officials conducted a thorough appraisal of the problem and considered reestablishing the Barrier Zone to prevent additional spread and reduce damage (Perry 1955) (Fig. 1.3). The plan was implemented to the extent allowed by available funds but was eventually discontinued. In 1956, the Congress made funds available to initiate an eradication program; 2,230 km² in three states were sprayed with DDT, which had been used experimentally from 1944 to 1948 in Pennsylvania; another 12,000 km² were sprayed in 1957. By 1958, less than 0.5 km² of defoliation was recorded within the generally infested area (Gypsy Moth Dig. 2005); however, the use of DDT was curtailed because of concerns about its bioaccumulation in food and feed crops and detrimental effects on beneficial organisms, fish, and wildlife. Hopes for eradication were then abandoned and a long-overdue emphasis was placed on research.

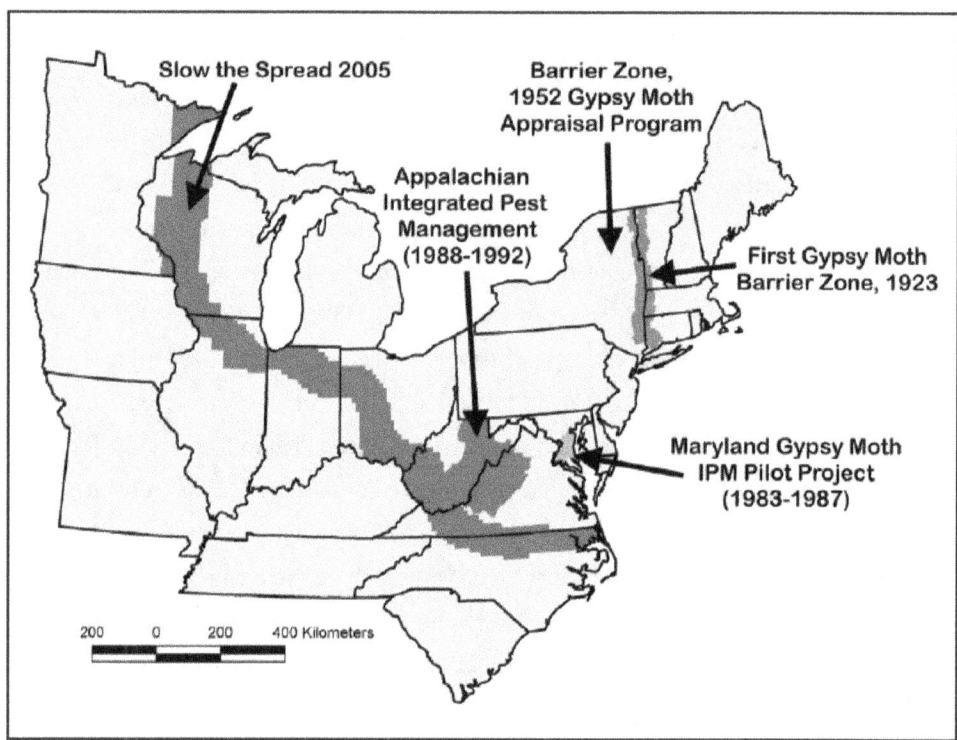

Figure 1.3.—*Locations of barrier zones and IPM programs targeting the spread of gypsy moth in the United States.*

Emphasis on Gypsy Moth Research

The areas of infestation and defoliation increased substantially between 1959 and 1969, providing impetus for an accelerated program of research on the gypsy moth that began in 1971 when the USDA redirected $1 million to the Forest Service and the Agricultural Research Service. This was timely because gypsy moth infestations worsened regionally as more than 8,000 km² were defoliated in 1971. The Congress provided a special annual appropriation of $2.4 million to the USDA over a 4-year period (1975-78) to accelerate research and development (R&D) on gypsy moth (McManus 1978). The need to develop an integrated pest management (IPM) approach was recognized early in the planning stages and remained a central theme throughout the period of accelerated R&D. Many of the technologies currently used to monitor and control gypsy moth populations were developed during this period.

In 1978, program management initiated a contract with Ketron, Inc. to develop a cost/benefit analysis for "gypsy moth containment." The report (Blacksten et al. 1978) concluded that significant expenditures were justified even to slow the spread of the gypsy moth into the uninfested states. The report also emphasized that a containment strategy must include efforts to detect and eliminate the artificial introduction of life stages that occur annually beyond the generally infested area. This in itself would require a significant commitment of resources because during the next severe outbreak (1980-82), during which the gypsy moth defoliated more than 106,000 km², the State of California recorded more than 2,000 interceptions of gypsy moth life stages originating from 14 states and Canada in subsequent years. This documented the enormous potential for the artificial introduction of gypsy moth into states far removed from the generally infested area (McFadden and McManus 1991).

Change in Management Strategy: The IPM Approach

Since the 1960's, attempts to control the gypsy moth have varied greatly from state to state but have been primarily reactive, that is, aerial spraying was conducted in areas where defoliation had been observed in the previous year or was predicted to occur in the current year. This approach was used by states and municipalities to protect foliage and to alleviate the nuisance effect in urban residential areas. It was supported primarily by the USDA state and Federal cooperative suppression programs under guidelines developed by states individually and approved by the Forest Service. It became apparent that this approach was costly and provided only temporary relief from the insect and its impacts. Further, the public became sensitized to the potential adverse effects of pesticides to human health and to the environment.

Following the massive defoliation in 1981 (Fig. 1.2), it became apparent that there was a need to evaluate a more proactive approach to manage gypsy moth populations before they reached defoliating levels. In 1983, the first sustained attempt to manage the gypsy moth, embracing the concepts of integrated pest management (IPM), was initiated in Maryland. The Maryland Gypsy Moth IPM Pilot Project was a 5-year (1983-87) cooperative effort between the State Department of Agriculture and the State and Private Forestry branch of the Forest Service. The stated goal was to evaluate the feasibility of managing the gypsy moth at low levels over a wide range of ecological, geographical, and land-use areas (Reardon et al. 1987). The project encompassed a four-county area containing approximately 4,232 km², of which roughly 920 km² were forested (Fig. 1.3).

The project was structured around a comprehensive system of surveillance and biological monitoring designed to provide an annual baseline on the distribution and abundance of gypsy moth populations and their natural enemies. A monitoring system consisting of pheromone-baited traps and larval sampling devices was overlaid throughout the project area on a fixed-point grid (1 km) established on Universal Transverse Mercator (UTM) coordinates. A database management system was developed by which optical scanning technology was used to collate monitoring data from more than 1,800 fixed-grid points within the project area. This system facilitated efficient processing of all data and produced timely and practical displays of tables and maps that were used by managers to identify areas where more intensive egg-mass surveys or suppression treatments should be conducted in the following year (Roberts et al. 1993).

Although the benefits of preventive treatments were not demonstrated during the 5-year project, several notable outcomes were recorded. The project was successful in reducing low-density gypsy moth populations and in identifying the need to develop additional technologies, such as biopesticides, for use in environmentally sensitive areas. The Maryland IPM Pilot Project also provided a demonstration of the IPM concept over a regional scale. The advantages derived from maintaining a fixed-point monitoring system for gypsy moth also were apparent. Areas where gypsy moth populations were increasing rapidly ("hot spots") were readily identified and labor-intensive egg-mass surveys were allocated only to areas where these were significant trend changes.

A series of meetings attended by state and Federal officials was initiated in 1986 to discuss the desirability and feasibility of conducting a management program along the "leading edge" of the generally infested zone to impede the spread of the insect to uninfested states. The leading edge was defined as the interface or transition zone between where the gypsy moth occurs and where male moths usually are the only life stage that can be readily detected. In 1987, Congress directed the Forest Service to continue efforts to manage the leading edge of gypsy moth populations along the Allegheny Mountains in Virginia and West Virginia by initiating a 5-year special project (1988-92), the Appalachian Integrated Pest Management Gypsy Moth Project (AIPM), which encompassed 51,800 km^2 in 20 counties in West Virginia and 18 counties in Virginia (Fig. 1.3) (Reardon 1991; Ravlin et al. 1991, 1992).

Project objectives were to:
1. Minimize the spread and adverse effects of the gypsy moth.
2. Develop a prototype IPM structure consisting of standardized sampling protocols, decision matrices for intervention activities, computer-based geographic information systems (GIS), and an education program.
3. Evaluate intervention tactics for managing isolated and low-density populations.

4. Assess the feasibility of implementing a coordinated county, state, and Federal program over a large area.

The data management and monitoring systems were patterned after those used in the Maryland IPM Pilot Project, but the sampling grids ranged from 1 to 3 km because of the rough terrain common to the area. The project area was divided into four action zones with different management objectives and survey protocols that were determined by the proximity of sites to the generally infested zone, and by the average number of male moths recovered in grids of pheromone-baited traps (Reardon 1991). The AIPM Project was successful in developing a prototype IPM structure, implementing intervention activities through *a priori* decision rules, and developing technologies— particularly geospatial tools—for managing low-density gypsy moth infestations on a regional scale (Fleischer et al. 1992, Ravin et al. 1992, Roberts et al. 1993). It also demonstrated the use of GIS data for evaluating operational treatment effectiveness (Liebhold et al. 1996). A portion of the project area was designated for implementation of an area-wide approach to "slow the spread" of gypsy moth populations (Reardon 1996).

Rationale for Gypsy Moth Slow the Spread Program

Following the outbreaks of the 1980's and the surge in isolated infestations, there was grudging acceptance that the gypsy moth probably would continue to spread to the south and west until it eventually occupied the natural range of the oak-hickory and oak-pine forest types. It was recognized that a regional management program for the insect required collaboration at all levels of government, scientists, and managers, as well as a standardized system for monitoring and decision support (Ravlin et al. 1987; Ravlin 1991). It also was known that advances of the gypsy moth into the next tier of states beyond the leading edge of the generally infested zone would greatly increase costs associated with managing the insect, and magnify proportionally the area from which inadvertent introductions can emanate (McFadden and McManus 1991).

Much was at stake in the next tier of states. In Tennessee, Kentucky, and Missouri, an early appraisal documented that 50 to 80 percent of the forested land in those states was classified as highly susceptible to gypsy moth damage based on proportion of favored food species present, dry sites, poor stocking densities, and history of abuse (Perry 1955).

In November, 1988, the National Plant Board facilitated a meeting of state and Federal officials in Raleigh, North Carolina, to address the feasibility of establishing a program to "contain" gypsy moth populations. A series of recommendations included charging the Animal and Plant Health Inspection Service (APHIS) to establish a uniform male-moth trapping survey within all states (50 percent cost share), and requesting that the USDA provide a cost/benefit analysis for a program to reduce the spread of, and/or containment of gypsy moth populations. For the first time, the concept of a "transition zone" was defined: "a contiguous area between the federally regulated zone and a distant point where no gypsy moth life stages are detected (except male moths), and where the pattern of moth catches indicates the possible presence of an infestation." As a result of this meeting, APHIS and the Forest Service developed a memorandum of understanding that defined responsibilities for assisting states in eradicating small isolated gypsy moth infestations on nonfederal lands; APHIS also increased the regulation of "outdoor household articles" that were responsible for about 90 percent of the 170 isolated infestations that had been detected in the late 1980's.

In 1990, William Leuschner, then at Virginia Polytechnic Institute and State University, was contracted by the Forest Service to estimate the general order of magnitude of benefits and costs that might be incurred in developing a program to contain the spread of the gypsy moth. Because of the urgency of this study, certain assumptions and approximations were made about demographics of human populations and the distribution of forest types within the geographical areas of interest. With the assistance of a team of technical experts, a scenario was developed that described what might happen within the next 25 years to the distribution and abundance of gypsy moth populations within the project area, and what activities and impacts would be realized with and without enactment of a containment project to slow the progression of spread. The details of this scenario are provided in the final report of the assessment (Leuschner 1991). By definition, a Gypsy Moth Containment Program (GMCP) would occur in a well-defined transition zone in which detection efforts are intensified and are similar to those that were deployed in the AIPM Demonstration Project. A grid of pheromone-baited traps would be placed on UTM coordinates at a spacing of 2 or 3 km as determined by the topography of the area. When small infestations are detected within the transition zone, more intensive grids of traps (250 to 500 m apart) would be used to delimit the infestations before their eventual treatment with environmentally acceptable tactics such as mating disruption or microbial pesticides.

The fundamental benefit of the proposed GMCP was to slow the rate of spread of the gypsy moth throughout the transition zone and into the uninfested zone and not to halt the spread of the insect. Further, activities within the GMCP were not designed to have an affect in the generally infested zone where populations are episodic and where management activities were expected to continue as warranted. The assessment was based on a spread simulation model that projected the spread of the gypsy moth through the transition zone at six different rates over a 25-year period, and an economic model that projected potential impacts caused by the gypsy moth in the affected areas over the same period for different rates of spread (Table 1.1). The difference in damages incurred with and without a GMCP was the estimated program benefit. This value was used to

Table 1.1.—*Negative impacts of gypsy moth over 25 years (1990-2015) when assuming historical spread rate of 20 km/yr (cf. Liebhold et al. 1992) and reduced spread rate of 12 km/yr (values in millions of U.S. dollars), and based on present values in 1990 (from table 2 in Leuschner et*

Activity or impact	Spread rate	
	20 km/yr	12 km/year
Management activities	158.5	92.9
Timber impacts	267.5	173.6
Recreational impacts	241.7	143.0
Residential impacts	3,131.1	1,820.7
Total	3,798.8	2,230.2

estimate how much money could be justified annually to implement a program designed to slow the spread of the gypsy moth. The assessment concluded that a midrange scenario in which the rate of spread was reduced from 20 to 8 km/year could justify an annual program expenditure of $19.2 million. In response to this economic assessment, and with the Forest Service intent to transition AIPM products and activities into their Forest Pest Management Program, a briefing paper was prepared in March, 1992, entitled "A strategy to evaluate technologies to slow the spread of the gypsy moth" (Ravlin et al. 1992). This concept was approved and in the summer of 1992 the Forest Service approved and initiated the STS Pilot Project with the following objectives:

1. Demonstrate that new and current technology can slow the rate of spread of gypsy moth populations.
2. Assess the technological, economic, ecological, and environmental viability of implementing an operational STS Program.
3. Implement a plan for integrating STS technology into a national strategy for gypsy moth management.

A Steering Committee was formed that consisted of representatives from the Forest Service, APHIS, and participating states that were responsible for project implementation. A Technical Committee consisting of scientists from the Forest Service, APHIS, and states and universities was charged with providing expert recommendations on the technical aspects of the project to the Steering Committee. The initial project area encompassed 21 counties in the states of North Carolina, Virginia, and West Virginia, and Federal lands contained therein. Portions of three counties in the Upper Peninsula of Michigan were added to the project area in 1993. The STS Pilot Project continued through FY 1999 and demonstrated that the rate of spread of the gypsy moth could be reduced by nearly 50 percent (Leonard and Sharov 1995). In FY 2000, STS became fully operational and today is considered a major component of a national strategy to manage the gypsy moth (Fig. 1.3). A historical perspective of the gypsy moth in the United States is projected in Table 1.2.

Table 1.2.—*Timeline of selected gypsy moth events in the United States, 1869-2005*

1869	Gypsy moths imported by Etienne Trouvelot escape from his home at 27 Myrtle Street in Medford, Massachusetts.
1870	Riley and Vasey (1870) published first report of presence of gypsy moth in North America.
1889	First major gypsy moth outbreak in the U.S., centering on Medford, Massachusetts.
1890	Massachusetts State Department of Agriculture allocates $25,000 to eradicate gypsy moth (March 14) at a time when low-skilled U.S. workers earn roughly 2¢ per hour (Riis 1890). First recorded use of a chemical pesticide (copper acetoarsenite, or Paris green) against the gypsy moth.
1892	Paris green replaced with lead arsenate to control gypsy moth.
1900	Massachusetts discontinues its gypsy moth eradication program.
1906	Congress appropriates funds to USDA to manage gypsy moth. Federal government and Massachusetts jointly fund exploration and importation of natural enemies for gypsy moth control.
1910–1911	*Entomophaga* complex introduced from Japan to control gypsy moth but fungal pathogen does not become established.
1912	Federal quarantine is implemented for gypsy moth to regulate potential movement of insect's life stages to new areas.
1920	Serious infestation (>1,000 km²) in Somerville, New Jersey, results from importation of infested blue spruce trees from The Netherlands.
1923	First barrier-zone management strategy against gypsy moth implemented from Canada to Long Island along Champlain and Hudson River Valleys.
1926	First aerial spray contract awarded for gypsy moth control on Cape Cod, Massachusetts.
1934	USDA begins to codify gypsy moth quarantine under the U.S. Code of Federal Regulations (Title 7, Chapter III, Section 301.45).
1941	Barrier zone implemented in 1923 discontinued in part due to reduction in funding caused by U.S. entry in World War II.
1944–1948	Use of DDT to control gypsy moth tested in Pennsylvania.
1945	Last use of lead arsenate to control gypsy moth.
1953	Reestablishment of barrier zone against gypsy moth along Adirondack Mountains in New York to Allegheny Plateau.
1955	C.C. Perry authors "Gypsy Moth. Appraisal Program and Proposed Plan to Prevent Spread of the Moths," which describes use of barrier zones to limit gypsy moth spread rate.
1956	Congress authorizes eradication program against gypsy moth.
1957	Height of DDT use against gypsy moth as more than 12,000 km² treated with pesticide.
1958	DDT phased out due to concerns about its toxicity. Replaced with carbaryl, which is used exclusively in ensuing years.
1968	Formation of National Gypsy Moth Council consisting of Federal and state agencies and other organizations. Council addresses escalating gypsy moth infestations and seeks funding for research and development.
1970	Gypsy moth sex pheromone (disparlure) correctly identified and isolated (Bierl et al. 1970) .
1971	USDA allocates $1 million for gypsy moth research when the median family income in United States exceeds $10,000 for the first time.
1972	First use of *Bacillus thuringiensis kurstaki* to control gypsy moth. DDT banned by U.S. Environmental Protection Agency. Beroza and Knipling (1972) propose gypsy moth control through use of pheromones to suppress mating. Mating disruption through applications of synthetic pheromone flakes later becomes dominant control tactic in STS Program.
1974	Congress funds "Big Bug" programs (gypsy moth, southern pine beetle, and Douglas-fir tussock moth) through special appropriation; programs are established under Secretary of Agriculture.
1975-1978	With funding of gypsy moth included as a "Big Bug" program, gypsy moth research and development expanded. More than $10 million allocated over 4 years, which results in much of the technology used today in STS and other gypsy moth management programs.

1976	Diflubenzuron (Dimilin®) registered by U.S. Environmental Protection Agency for use against gypsy moth.
1978	First published economic assessment of costs and benefits of gypsy moth containment program (Blacksten et al. 1978). Gypchek, commercial formulation of gypsy moth nucleopolyhedrosis virus, registered by the U.S. Environmental Protection Agency for use against gypsy moth. National Gypsy Moth Council restructured as National Gypsy Moth Management Board, which acts as coordinating body for all gypsy moth activities in the United States. First meeting of the National Gypsy Moth Review (later Annual Gypsy Moth Review).
1979	First operational use of synthetic pheromone flakes in Oconomowoc, Wisconsin, to suppress gypsy moth mating. National Gypsy Moth Management Board issues "The Comprehensive Gypsy Moth Management System."
1981	Six counties in Michigan placed under quarantine: Osceola, Midland, Isabella, Saginaw, Montcalm, and Gratiot. The infestation is spatially discontinuous from rest of quarantine area. Largest gypsy moth defoliation on record as more than 52,000 km² defoliated across 10-state area. USDA publishes "The Gypsy Moth: Research Towards Integrated Pest Management" (Doane and McManus 1981).
1983–1987	Maryland Gypsy Moth IPM Pilot Project implemented in Prince George, Anne Arundel, Calvert, and Charles Counties.
1988	Use of lead arsenate against gypsy moth banned by U.S. Environmental Protection Agency.
1988–1992	Appalachian Integrated Pest Management Program against gypsy moth implemented in 38-county area in West Virginia and Virginia.
1989	Epizootic of fungal pathogen *Entomophaga maimaiga* first detected in United States in Connecticut, New Hampshire, Vermont, Pennsylvania, New Jersey, and New York.
1990	First annual meeting of USDA Interagency Gypsy Moth Research Forum (later USDA Interagency Research Forum on Invasive Species).
1991	Economic assessment of costs and benefits of slowing spread of gypsy moth published (Leuschner 1991).
1992	First published quantitative assessment of historical spread of gypsy moth in United States (Liebhold et al. 1992). Major finding is that historical spread from 1966 to 1989 was 20.7 km/yr. Spread rate of 10 km/yr was set as goal for the STS Program. Appalachian Integrated Pest Management Program discontinued. Ravlin et al. (1992) detail evaluation of technologies for slowing gypsy moth spread and describe framework upon which Decision Algorithm is developed.
1992–1998	STS Pilot Project initiated in Virginia, West Virginia, North Carolina, and Michigan.
1999	STS integrated with USDA's national strategy for managing gypsy moth.
2000	Gypsy Moth Slow the Spread Foundation Inc., formed to manage STS Program, initially comprises officials from North Carolina, Virginia, West Virginia, Indiana, Illinois, Michigan, and Wisconsin.
2003	Most extensive use of mating disruption tactics to date as more than 2,270 km² treated with synthetic pheromone flakes.
2005	560 counties in the United States are currently under quarantine for gypsy moth.

Chapter 2. Population Biology of Gypsy Moth Spread

Andrew M. Liebhold[1], Alexei A. Sharov[2], and Patrick C. Tobin[1]

Introduction

The gypsy moth in North America (Elkinton and Liebhold 1990) is one example of a much larger problem, namely, ever increasing biological invasions. Over the last 50 years, the forests of Eastern North America have been particularly afflicted by a multitude of alien insects and diseases. Many of these have substantially altered ecosystem properties and processes (Liebhold et al. 1995). Given the magnitude of this problem we need to understand the population processes operating during biological invasions. The development of such an understanding is a prerequisite for developing strategies for managing current and future invasions.

Biological invasions can be divided into three distinct population processes: arrival (the process by which individuals are transported from their native to an exotic habitat); establishment (the process by which populations grow to sufficient levels that extinction no longer is likely); and spread (the expansion of a population's range in the exotic region) (Dobson and May 1986, Liebhold et al. 1995, Shigesada and Kawasaki 1997, Natl. Res. Counc. 2002). Corresponding to each of these invasion phases is a management activity: 1) international quarantines and inspections are strategies for preventing arrival, 2) detection and eradication are activities for preventing establishment, and 3) domestic quarantines and barrier zones are strategies for limiting the spread of alien species.

The gypsy moth is an excellent species for illustrating the population processes operating during biological invasions. The first arrival of the gypsy moth occurred many years ago; the accidental release of gypsy moth occurred in 1868 or 1869 in the Boston suburb of Medford by an amateur entomologist, Etienne Léopold Trouvelot (see Chapter 1). Despite early efforts to eradicate the gypsy moth, the insect was firmly established in the Boston area by 1900. Due to the limited dispersal capability of the European gypsy moth strain (Trouvelot is thought to have released a European strain in which females are incapable of flight), gypsy moth spread in North America has been slow. Over the last century it has invaded less than a third of its potential range (Sharov and Liebhold 1998b, Morin et al. 2004). This prolonged period of spread has provided considerable

---

[1] USDA Forest Service, Northern Research Station, 180 Canfield Street, Morgantown, West Virginia 26505.
[2] Laboratory of Genetics, National Institute on Aging (NIA/NIH), 333 Cassell Drive, Suite 3000, Baltimore, Maryland 21224.

time to study gypsy moth spread and the vast quantity of data collected on gypsy moth dynamics at the expanding population front has led to an extensive understanding of the spread of this insect, perhaps better than any other alien species.

Introduction to the Population Ecology of Biological Invasions

Not every seed that falls to the ground becomes a tree. Similarly, of the many insect invaders that arrive in a new habitat, few become established. Founder populations typically are small and consequently are at great risk of extinction from both direct effects such as disturbance and indirect effects such as the highly restricted genetic variability in founding populations. Generally, the smaller the founder population, the less likely the insect will become established (MacArthur and Wilson 1967, Mollison et al. 1986). This relationship is clearly illustrated by historical records of introductions of natural enemies as part of biological control programs; establishment frequencies are consistently higher from releases of large numbers of individuals (Beirne 1975, Fagan et al. 2002).

Much of what we know about the population biology of low-density invading populations is extracted from a rich literature on the population ecology of rare species, i.e., conservation biology. All populations are affected by stochastic abiotic influences, e.g., weather, but low-density populations are particularly sensitive to perturbation. We can mathematically represent the generational change, from t to $t+1$, in population density as

$$N_{t+1} = f(N_t) + \varepsilon_t , \qquad\qquad (2.1)$$

where N_t is population density in year t, $f(N_t)$ is a function that encompasses birth and death processes, and ε_t is variation due to environmental stochasticity. The important result of demographic and environmental stochasticity is that low-density populations, e.g., newly founded invading populations, are particularly prone to extinction as a result of this random variation. However, another factor contributing to extinction of low-density populations must be considered: Allee dynamics.

Warder Allee (1932) studied animal population ecology and generally is recognized as the first worker to recognize a phenomenon in low-density populations of most species, that is, certain processes may lead to decreasing net population growth with decreasing density. As a result of this relationship, there sometimes is a threshold below which low-density populations are driven toward extinction (Fig. 2.1). This phenomenon, called the Allee effect, can result from one of many biological mechanisms, for example, an Allee effect could be due to insufficient cooperative feeding or a failure to find mates at low densities (Courchamp et al. 1999). The Allee effect has been identified as critical

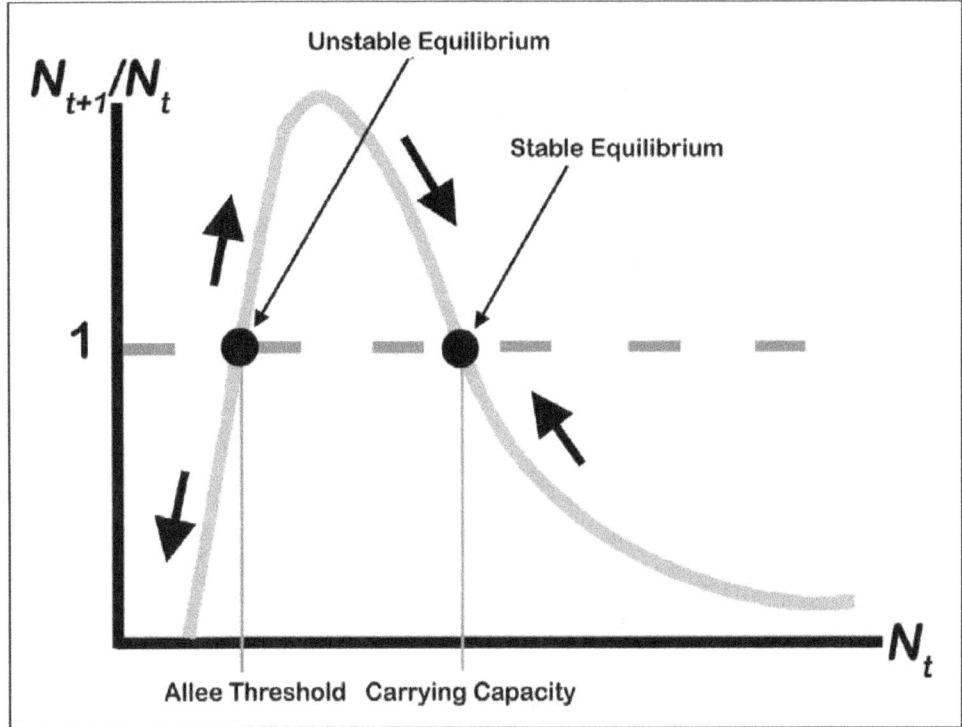

Figure 2.1.—*Schematic of the Allee effect. Change in population density, N_{t+1} / N_t is plotted as a function of density at the beginning of the generation, N_t. This relationship determines change in population density $f(N_t)$ shown in equation 2.1. Note that when density is greater than the minimum population density, it will increase or decrease toward the stable equilibrium, but when it is below this threshold, density will decrease toward extinction.*

in understanding patterns of extinction from the perspective of conservation biology (Stephens and Sutherland 1999), and there is growing recognition of its important role during the establishment phase of biological invasions (Drake 2004, Leung et al. 2004, Johnson et al. 2006, Tobin et al. 2007b). The magnitude of the Allee effect varies greatly among species due to variation in life history traits. However, virtually every sexually reproducing species can be expected to exhibit an Allee effect at low densities. As such, Allee dynamics may be of critical importance in understanding why some species establish more easily than others.

Understanding the establishment process has important implications for management. The activity we call "eradication" is aimed at reversing the process of establishment; eradication is forced extinction (Myers et al. 2000). It follows from the previous description that eradication is likely to succeed only in situations in which the target population is both low in density and highly restricted in its spatial distribution. Liebhold and Bascompte (2003) used an Allee effect model to illustrate the numerical relationships between initial numbers of individuals, the strength of an eradication treatment (percent killed), and the probability of population persistence.

Once a population is established, its density typically will increase and individuals will disperse into adjoining areas of suitable habitat. Three phases to the range expansion process are generally recognized (Shigesada and Kawasaki 1997) (Fig. 2.2). Following establishment of the alien population, there is an initial period during which spread accelerates. In the early stages of this phase, populations may remain at extremely low densities and, therefore, remain undetected for several years (Kean and Barlow 2000). The bulk of range expansion occurs during the expansion phase. During this phase, the radial rate of spread often increases linearly, but in other cases it may accelerate in a nonlinear fashion (Andow et al. 1990). Finally, as the expanding range begins to saturate the geographic extent of suitable habitat, spread declines and ultimately stops.

The spread of a population is driven by two processes: population growth and dispersal. As a result, most models of population spread have focused on these processes. The simplest and probably the most widely applied model of population spread was developed by Skellam (1951). This model combined random (Gaussian) dispersal with exponential (Malthusian) population growth to model expansion following an initial introduction of N individuals at time $t=0$, and at location $x=0$ and $y=0$, denoted as $N_{0,0,0}$. The number of individuals at a distance x and y, and time t, from the initial site of introduction is given by

$$N_{x,y,t} = \frac{N_{0,0,0}}{4\pi Dt} e^{\left(rt - \frac{x^2+y^2}{4Dt}\right)}, \tag{2.2}$$

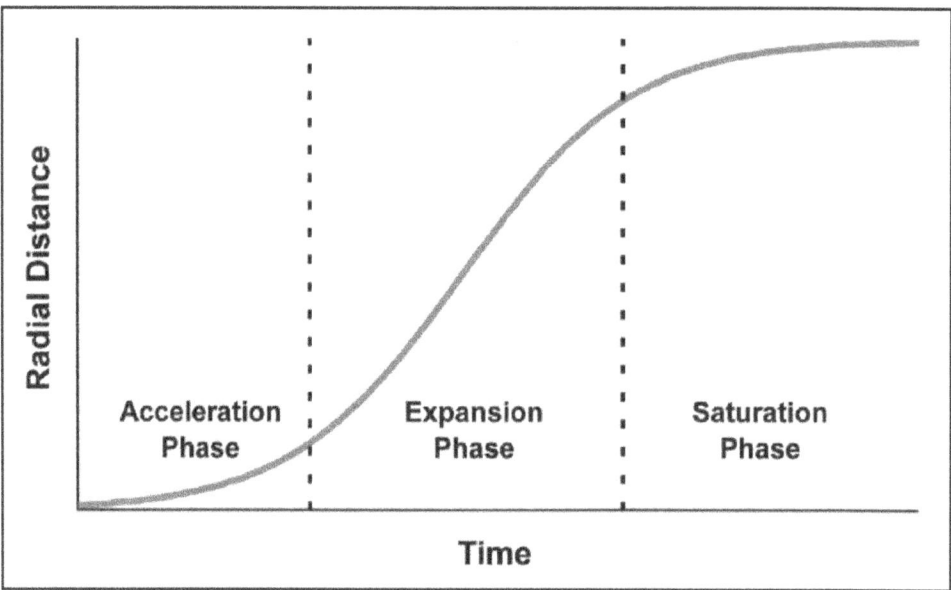

Figure 2.2.—*Generalized range expansion of invading species. Radial distance refers to the distance from the site of introduction to the expanding population front.*

where D is the "diffusion coefficient" (a measure of the amount of movement) and r is the intrinsic rate of increase from the exponential growth model and is a measure of population growth under ideal conditions. The assumption of random movement in this model implies that the population will spread radially at an equal rate in all directions (Fig. 2.3A). Skellam (1951) showed that for any detection threshold, T, such that the infested area at any time t is restricted to points where $N_{x,t} > T$, the expansion velocity of the infested front (radial rate of spread), V, is constant and can be described:

$$V = 2\sqrt{rD} .$$
(2.3)

This model assumes that r and D are constant through time and space during the period of range expansion of the invading organism, an assumption that intuitively seems unlikely, e.g., spatial variation in the habitat may profoundly affect birth/death functions as well as dispersal rates. Nevertheless, there has generally been some (but not total) congruence between predictions of this model and observed rates of spread of most exotic organisms (Andow et al. 1990, Shigesada and Kawasaki 1997).

Fisher (1937) advanced a nearly identical model to that of Skellam (1951) except that he assumed population growth had finite limits represented by a logistic growth model versus the exponential model. Interestingly, the asymptotic wave speed in the Fisher model is identical to that of the Skellam model (eq. 2.3). This similarity of spread behavior reflects the fact that range expansion in both models is driven by population growth near the expanding population front; population growth in areas that have been infested for many years has little effect on spread. A mathematical exploration of general conditions leading to constant rates of spread is found in Weinberger et al. (2002).

Skellam's model assumes a single, continuous form of dispersal and predicts that range expansion should be a smooth, continuous process (Fig. 2.3a). However some species may be able to disperse in at least two ways. The existence of two forms of dispersal is referred to as "stratified dispersal" (Hengeveld 1989); in those situations, range expansion will proceed through the formation of multiple discrete, isolated colonies established ahead of the infested front (Shigesada et al. 1995, Shigesada and Kawasaki 1997). These colonies, in turn, will expand their range and ultimately coalesce. The result of this phenomenon is that range expansion may occur much faster than would occur under a more simple diffusion model. This pattern of spread through coalescing colonies also has been represented mathematically by applying spread models that incorporate dispersal kernels with "fat tails" (Clark et al. 2001), that is, there is an increased chance of relatively long-distance dispersal events.

There are many examples of invasive species that spread according to a coalescing colony model (Shigesada and Kawasaki 1997). Interesting aspects of this type of spread are that establishment is an important component, isolated colonies are formed ahead of the expanding population front due to dispersal of propagules (Fig. 2.3b), and the ability of these propagules to successfully initiate new populations that spread and coalesce is entirely dependent on their ability to establish successfully. Therefore, all of the population processes that are important to establishment, namely, stochasticity and Allee dynamics, may be of critical importance to the spread process. For example, the existence of a strong Allee effect will reduce probabilities of establishment, which, in turn, may reduce rates of spread (Lewis and Kareiva 1993). Studying the historical spread of the house finch in North America, Veit and Lewis (1996) found that mating success in isolated, low-density populations is low, and that this results in a strong Allee effect. Veit and Lewis (1996) modeled this effect and showed that Allee dynamics was of critical importance in explaining observed rates of spread.

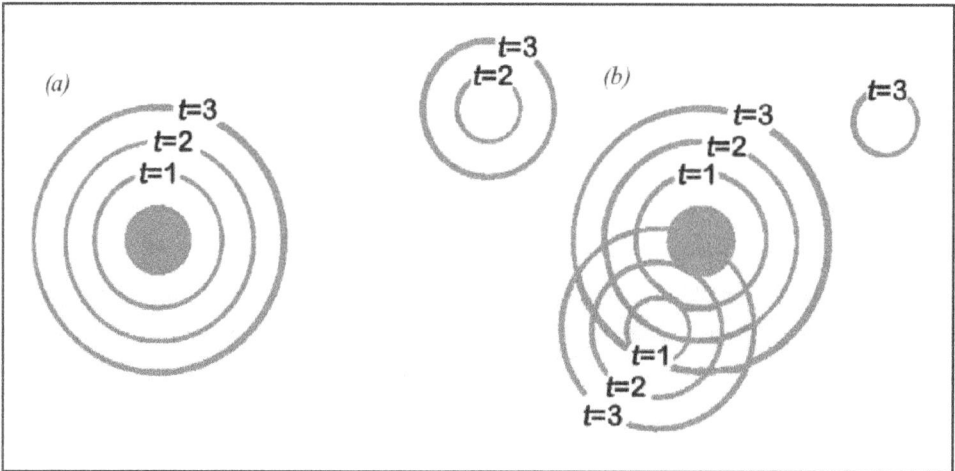

Figure 2.3.—*Schematic of range spread between successive generations. The solid red circle represents the initial range at time 0: (a) shows spread according to Skellam's (1951) model of successive time steps; (b) illustrates spread predicted using a stratified dispersal model (Hengeveld 1989, Shigesada et al. 1995, Shigesada and Kawasaki 1997).*

Gypsy Moth Spread: The "Big Picture"

As stated in Chapter 1, efforts to eradicate gypsy moth from Boston, Massachusetts, were abandoned by 1900; at that time, populations existed in parts of three counties in the greater Boston area. Over the next 100 years, the intensity of efforts to retard the spread of gypsy moth in North America varied. Through most of this period, there were considerable efforts to delimit the geographical extent of invading populations. As early as 1896, the production of chemical attractants by females was recognized and traps baited with live females were being utilized as powerful tools for detecting low-density, newly invaded populations (Forbush and Fernald 1896). By the 1940's, state and Federal agencies had discovered that the pheromone could be extracted from adult females and used as lures in traps. In 1970, the compound disparlure was isolated and ultimately synthesized for use as lures in thousands of traps (Bierl et al. 1970).

The continual use of pheromone-baited traps for detecting new gypsy moth infestations provides some historical consistency in records of gypsy moth range expansion. Unfortunately, records from most traps deployed prior to 1980 were not archived. Thus, our only source of historical information on the range expansion of gypsy moth over long periods (prior to 1980) and over the entire expanding population front (except perhaps excluding Canada) are records of when individual counties first became infested. Beginning with the enactment of the Domestic Plant Quarantine act of 1912, the U.S. Department of Agriculture (USDA) has listed (in the annual Code of Federal Regulations Title 7, chapter 301.45-2a) all counties that comprise the generally infested area (Weber 1930).

County-level maps of gypsy moth spread illustrate historical spread over the last 100 years (Fig. 2.4). While initial spread from 1900 to 1915 was primarily to the north, most of the spread since that time has been to the west and south. At the county level, spread appears as a continuous process; with the exception of Michigan, the range has always expanded into adjacent counties rather than "jumping" to outlying locations. The lone exception to this pattern is the population that apparently started in Midland, Michigan; populations were first detected there in the 1950's, but six counties were

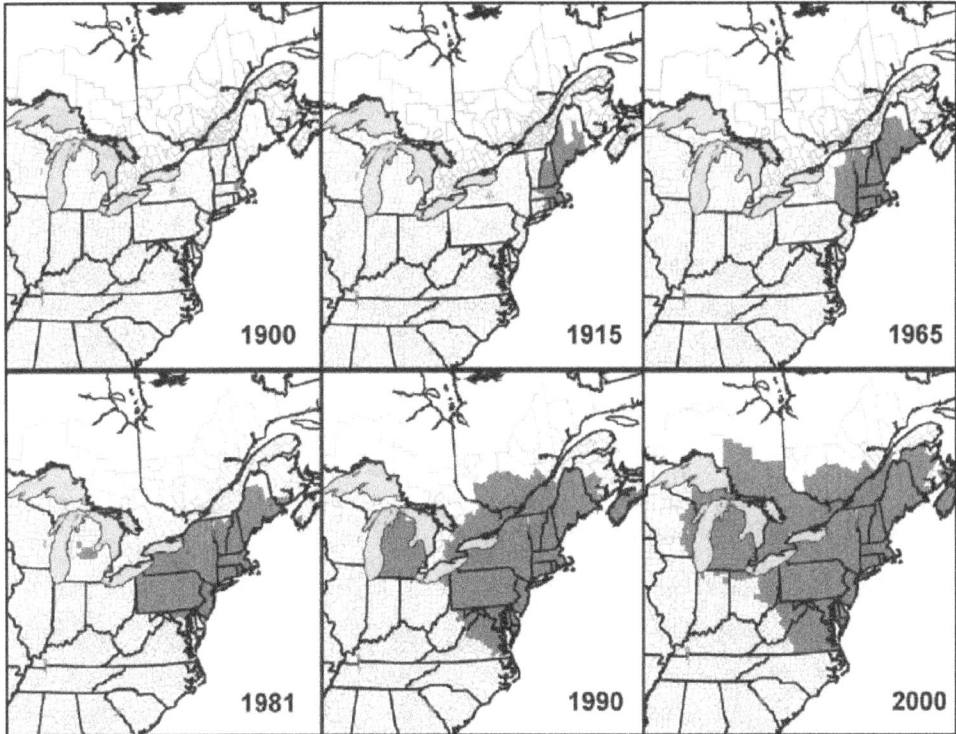

Figure 2.4.—*Historical gypsy moth spread in North America.*

infested by 1981 due to failed eradication efforts. This secondary focus has accelerated gypsy moth spread into much of the Midwest and spread from this focus now comprises a large proportion of the area infested (Fig. 2.5).

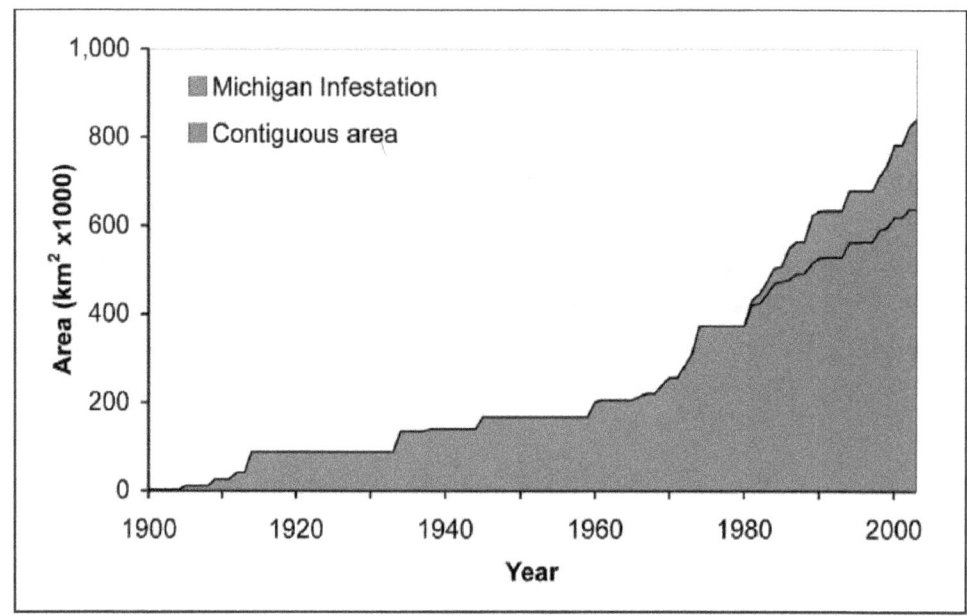

Figure 2.5.—*Historical increase in the geographical extent of established gypsy moth populations in North America based on quarantine records (cf. Liebhold et al. 1992, Tobin et al. 2007a).*

Liebhold et al. (1992) analyzed the historical spread of the gypsy moth in North America (both the United States and Canada) from 1900 to 1989 using historical county-level records of the advancing quarantine. By plotting the year of first establishment (quarantine) over the minimum distance from the point of introduction (Medford; calculated in a GIS), they were able to estimate the radial rate of range expansion as the slope of the linear model fit to this relationship using linear regression. Exploration of the data indicated that the rate of range expansion had varied through time and space (Table 2.1). Liebhold et al. (1992) speculated that the extremely slow rate of spread from 1916 to 1965 most likely was due to the implementation of a barrier zone in and around the Hudson River Valley during that time (see Chapter 1). Although this program apparently failed to stop the spread, it appears to have succeeded in slowing it. Liebhold et al. (1992) also found that from 1966 to 1989, spread rates in cold, northern climates were less than half those in the more temperate areas to the south. They attributed these lower rates of spread to lower population growth rates caused by severe overwintering mortality that is known to occur in extremely cold winter temperatures (e.g., Madrid and Stewart 1981).

Table 2.1.—*Radial rates of gypsy moth range expansion, 1900-1989, reported in Liebhold et al. (1992) and estimated from historical county-level quarantine records*

Interval	County subset	Number of counties	Radial rate of range expansion
			km/yr
1900–1915	All	52	9.45 ± 0.76
1916–1965	All	48	2.82 ± 0.19
1966–1989	Temperature < 7 °C[a]	225	7.61 ± 0.49
1966–1989	Temperature ≥ 7 °C[a]	98	20.78 ± 0.33

[a] Mean minimum January temperature.

Liebhold et al. (1992) compared these empirically derived estimates of spread rate with rates predicted from gypsy moth life-history traits. They used Skellam's (1951) equation (eq. 3.3) to estimate the expected spread rate under natural dispersal. Their estimates of r and D were derived from previously published demographic studies of population growth and dispersal (through windborne movement of first instars) and yielded an expected spread rate of ca. 2.5 km/yr. Since this rate falls far below the ca. 21 km/yr spread rate observed from 1966 to 1989 along most of the expanding gypsy moth population front, they concluded that the higher rates of spread must be due to the enhanced movement of gypsy moth through the accidental movement of life stages. Indeed, the behavior of late-instar gypsy moth, in which they seek cryptic resting places, frequently results in the inadvertent transport of life stages on vehicles and other manmade objects (McFadden and McManus 1991, Liebhold et al. 1994).

Gypsy Moth Spread: The "Close-up Picture"

Although the historical quarantine records described are the only data available for examining gypsy moth spread over long periods, they are problematic in that designations of quarantines are not always based on objective biological data, and county-level records do not provide very detailed spatial information about spread. As early as the 1890's (Forbush and Fernald 1896), pheromone-baited traps were used to monitor the spread of gypsy moth populations. In early efforts, traps were baited with live females; later, extracts of pheromone glands were used. The chemical structure of the attractant disparlure was identified in 1970 (Bierl et al. 1970) and the enhanced activity of the (+) enantiomer was not recognized until later (Iwaki et al. 1974, Mori et al. 1976). The standardization of trap designs (see Chapter 3) did not occur until the mid-1970's, and the concept of deploying large numbers of traps in a grid to characterize the advancing population front was not implemented until the early 1980's (see Chapter 1) (Reardon et al. 1987, 1993). As part of various intensified programs to manage gypsy moth along the expanding population front, grids of traps have been deployed along the transition zone since the mid-1980's and the data obtained are a useful resource for furthering our understanding of gypsy moth spread. The central Appalachian region has the longest history of intensified trapping but since the STS Program became a multistate effort, trapping has been extended along the entire population front. Currently, 70,000 to 90,000 traps are deployed annually as part of the program (see Table 3.1).

The United States can be divided into a generally infested area, i.e., gypsy moth populations are established, an uninfested area, i.e., populations are not established, or a "transition zone" between the two (Fig. 2.6). Male gypsy moths can sense small concentrations of disparlure (Leonhardt et al. 1996) and traps baited with (+) disparlure can detect newly established populations at low densities. Grids of traps deployed over large landscapes in the transition zone are powerful tools for characterizing the shape and dynamics of the advancing population front.

The development and use of mathematical algorithms to interpret male moth counts from trapping grids and estimate the boundaries of advancing populations is a critical component of the STS Decision Algorithm. See Chapter 5 as well as Sharov et al. (1996b, 1997b), and Tobin et al. (2004). This method can be used to identify boundaries

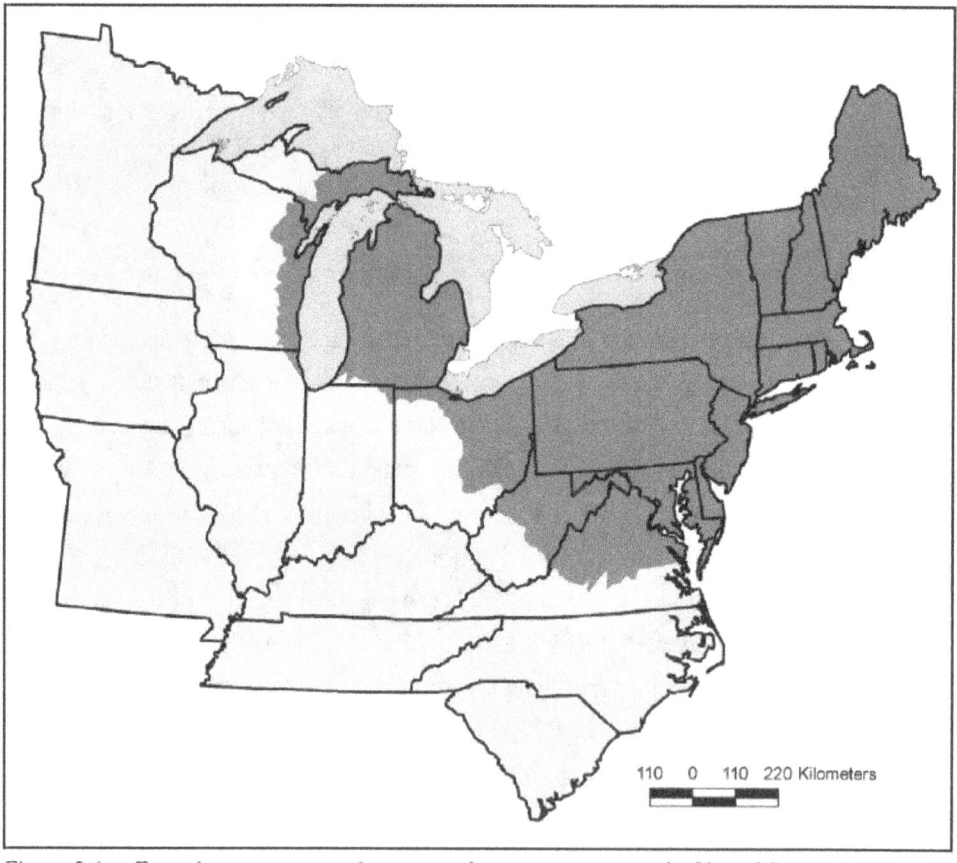

Figure 2.6.—*From the perspective of gypsy moth range expansion, the United States can be divided into the generally infested area (red), uninfested area (gray), and transition zone (yellow) as of 2000.*

corresponding to various gypsy moth population levels measured in spatially referenced traps, e.g., 1, 3, 10, ..., and 300 moths per trap, populations measured using standard egg mass sampling procedures, e.g., 1, 3, 10, ..., and 100 egg masses/1-ha plot, and populations evaluated based on aerial surveys for the presence of defoliation (Fig. 2.7). These results indicate that there is a type of gradation in gypsy moth abundance in the transition area. At the most distal portion, gypsy moth populations are absent as there were no captures in the majority of traps. But as one moves proximally toward the generally infested area, there is a zone of increasing numbers of positive trap catches. The point at which populations are present in nearly every location (one moth/trap line reaches unity in figure 2.7b) roughly corresponds with the 50th percentile of the 10 moths/ trap line. For this reason, and because it is the most stable boundary (Sharov et al. 1997b), the 10 moths/trap line is a useful definition of the advancing population front. However, one still must move even more toward the infested region before reaching an area at which egg masses can be detected by standard sampling methods (Fig. 2.7b). It is for this reason that egg mass sampling is not considered effective for assessing populations in the transition area even though it is the primary method for evaluating populations in

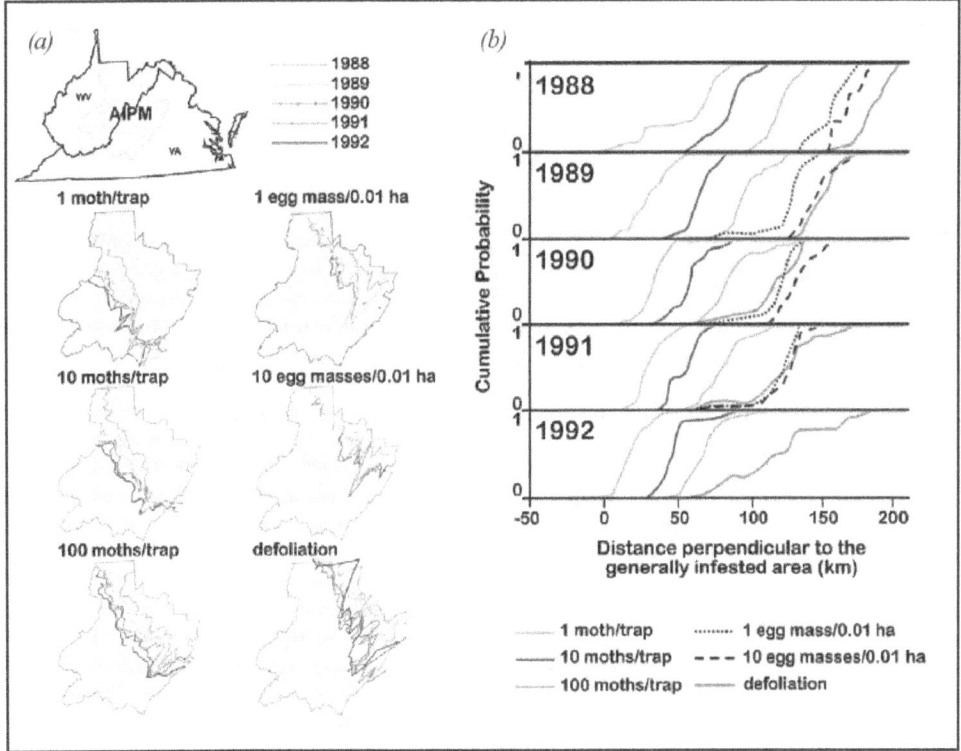

Figure 2.7.—*Population boundaries estimated from trapping grids located in the Appalachian Integrated Pest Management Program area in the central Appalachians, 1988-92: (a) maps of boundaries, and (b) distribution of boundary locations perpendicular to the general boundary direction (modified from figures 2 and 3 in Sharov et al. 1996b).*

suppression programs. Finally, located even deeper into the infested region is the area in which outbreak populations (detected through aerial surveys for defoliation) occur.

An important use of population boundaries is the estimation of spread rates based on the distance between boundaries in successive years (see Chapter 5) (Sharov et al. 1997b). Estimation of spread rates from trap data in this manner provides much more precision in space and time than estimates of spread rates from the county-level quarantine information described earlier (Tobin et al. 2007a). Yearly estimates of spread from trap data indicate that spread rates can vary considerably from year to year (Sharov et al. 1997b). Analysis of spread from trapping data collected in the central Appalachian region from 1984 through 1995 indicated that from 1984 to 1989, spread rates ranged from 17 to 30 km/yr. This is in approximate agreement with the 21 km/yr spread rate estimated from 1966 to 1989 by Liebhold et al. (1992) from county-level data. According to Sharov et al. (1997b), spread rates in this region after 1989 fell to an average of about 9 km/yr. They concluded that this decrease in spread resulted from containment activities conducted as part of the AIPM and STS Programs (see Chapter 1).

Another important characteristic of populations in the transition zone is their characteristic spatial aggregation. Sharov et al. (1996a) found that trap captures in the transition zone (defined as the area between the 1 and 300 moths/trap boundaries) were highly spatially autocorrelated, indicating the existence of "clumps" of elevated trap capture. The existence of these clumps in the transition area can be seen in Figure 2.8. Most of these clumps are thought to represent isolated populations that are formed ahead of the advancing population front. Thus, the spread of the gypsy moth appears to be an example of stratified dispersal as described previously. Isolated colonies are formed when propagules occasionally disperse well beyond the infested front. Populations in these colonies grow and eventually coalesce (Fig. 2.9a). Presumably, the mechanism of short-range, continuous dispersal that causes the growth of isolated populations is windborne dispersal of first instars (Mason and McManus 1981), and the mechanism behind the stochastic, long-range colony formation is accidental movement of life stages by humans (McFadden and McManus 1991). The potential role of long-range movement of gypsy moth life stages through meteorological events such as wind is still unknown. Sharov and Liebhold (1998a) used trap-grid data collected over several years from the transition area in the central Appalachians and were able to objectively identify isolated colonies and thereby estimate their rate of formation (Fig. 2.9b). They found that the rate of colony formation was around 70 per km^2 at a distance of 100 km from the defoliating front and then declined linearly to near zero at a distance of 250 km from the front. However, low levels of colony formation continued distally as far as their data extended. Indeed, isolated colonies are detected every year well beyond the expanding population front, even as far as Washington State (Liebhold and Bascompte 2003), though state and Federal eradication efforts generally are successful in eliminating them. The formation of these isolated colonies in the transition area is a possible explanation for spread rates that historically have greatly exceeded the predictions (Liebhold et al. 1992) of spread based on first-instar dispersal in Skellam's equation.

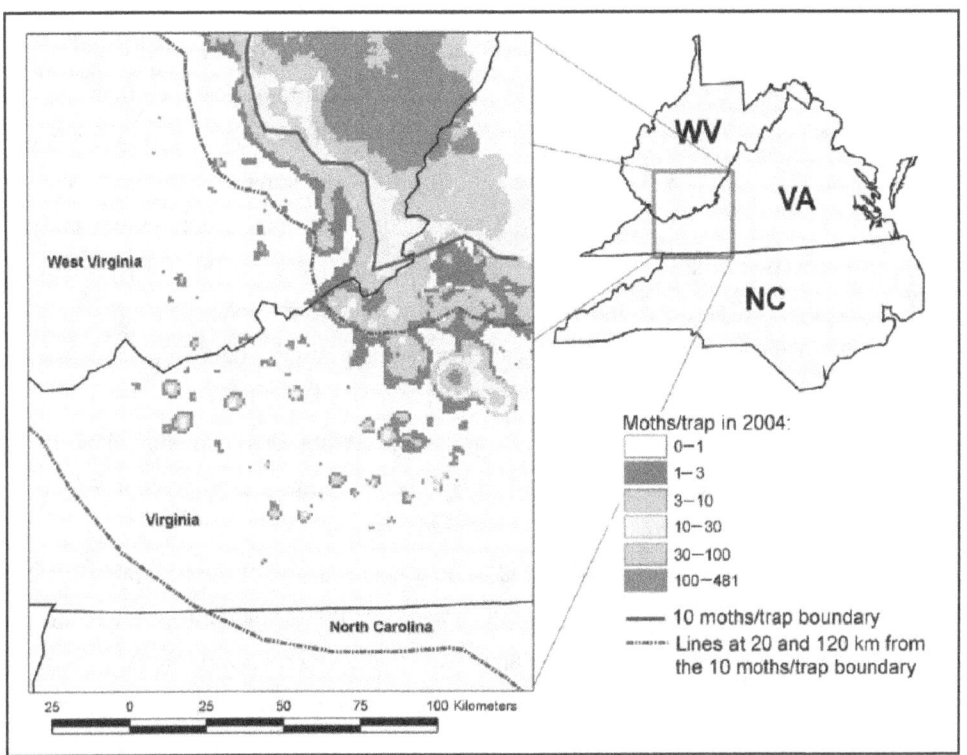

Figure 2.8.—*Trap capture of male moths interpolated from grids in the central Appalachians in 2004. Note the isolated colonies in the transition zone and ahead of the generally infested area.*

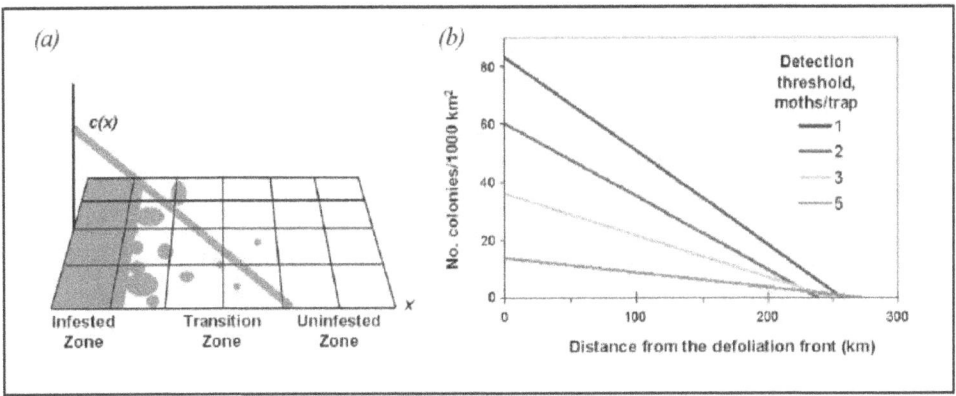

Figure 2.9.—*Colonization of isolated populations as a function of the distance* (x) *from the population front: (a) Colonization rates,* c(x), *decline over distance; (b) Colonization rates estimated from trap grids in the central Appalachians (modified from figure 9 in Sharov and Liebhold 1998a).*

Sharov and Liebhold (1998a) used the linear approximation of colony formation (Fig. 2.9) to model range expansion of the gypsy moth and predict the effectiveness of containment efforts. The model was inspired by the coalescing colony model (Shigesada and Kawasaki 1997), but instead of assuming a constant "jump distance" for colony formation, the model simulated variable jump distances. The rate of colony formation declined linearly with distance from the infested front (Fig. 2.9). The model of Sharov and Liebhold (1998a) combined colony formation in the transition area with colony growth and ultimate coalescence. They then used this model to predict the effect of various barrier-zone management activities. Specifically, they assumed that over some band of a specific width in the transition zone, all isolated colonies would be detected and eradicated. The model predicted that a barrier zone that was 100 km wide would result in a reduction in the radial rate of spread by about 50 percent. In the STS Program, there is no "control" so the actual effectiveness of the program cannot be evaluated directly. Nevertheless, over the last 10 years that the program has been in place in the central Appalachians, the radial rate of spread has averaged well below 10 km/yr, or nearly half of the historical average of 21 km/yr measured by Liebhold et al. (1992) from 1966 to 1989. Thus, the program appears to be exceeding the 50-percent reduction predicted by the model of Sharov and Liebhold (1998a).

We now know that the formation of isolated colonies ahead of the generally infested front is a central mechanism in gypsy moth spread. It is the formation of these colonies that causes spread to greatly exceed the approximate 2.5 km/yr spread rate that would be expected by continuous spread and first-instar dispersal in Skellam's model (Liebhold et al. 1992). Further, the entire strategy of the STS Program is built on the concept of finding isolated colonies (using grids of traps) and eliminating or retarding their growth. Despite the importance of colony formation, there are many unresolved questions about this process. Foremost among them is what mechanism(s) leads to colony formation? To iterate, life stages are constantly moved ahead of the infested front on objects such as firewood, timber, and motor vehicles, but the relative importance of these various pathways remains unknown. Certain types of long-distance dispersal of life stages, e.g., through wind, could contribute to colony formation but this has not been documented.

Because populations are initially isolated and sparse, it rarely is possible to observe the initial colonization event. Instead, we expect that colonization usually goes unnoticed and that some time must pass for colonies to grow in population size and geographical extent before they are detected in trapping grids. Nevertheless, there is one important characteristic of the early stages of colony formation that seems to be universally true: most isolated colonies go extinct on their own with no intervention. This phenomenon can be seen both in data collected in the transition area (Whitmire and Tobin 2006) and in more distant portions of the uninfested area (Liebhold and Bascompte 2003). Both of these studies found that most isolated populations went extinct by the year following their detection and that the probability of population persistence increased with increasing abundance (measured by trap capture). This population behavior is indicative of an Allee effect and is a critical aspect of the dynamics of isolated populations.

There are several possible mechanisms that contribute to the observed Allee effect in low-density populations. For example, predation by generalist predators (mostly small mammals) has been recognized to be the major source of mortality affecting low-density gypsy moth populations (Campbell and Sloan 1977, Elkinton et al. 1996); this predation is characterized by a type II functional response (Elkinton et al. 2004) and, therefore, causes inverse density-dependent mortality which can be expected to cause an Allee effect (Courchamp et al. 1999). Failure to find a mate is another major contributor to the existence of an Allee effect in isolated gypsy moth populations. Studies in the transition area in both Virginia and Wisconsin indicate that in sparse, isolated gypsy moth populations, a high proportion of females goes unmated and that this proportion increases as the abundance of males, as measured by trap capture, decreases (Sharov et al. 1995a, Tcheslavskaia et al. 2002).

Females of the European strain of the gypsy moth that is present in North America are incapable of flight while males are much more mobile. However, a mark-recapture experiment with males in small trap grids indicated that few disperse great distances (Elkinton and Carde 1980). Despite these results, there is other evidence that large numbers of males occasionally disperse from high-density populations into trapping grids in the transition area. One piece of evidence is simply the spatial and temporal patterns of trap capture. For example, in Figure 2.10 we see that in 1996 there were

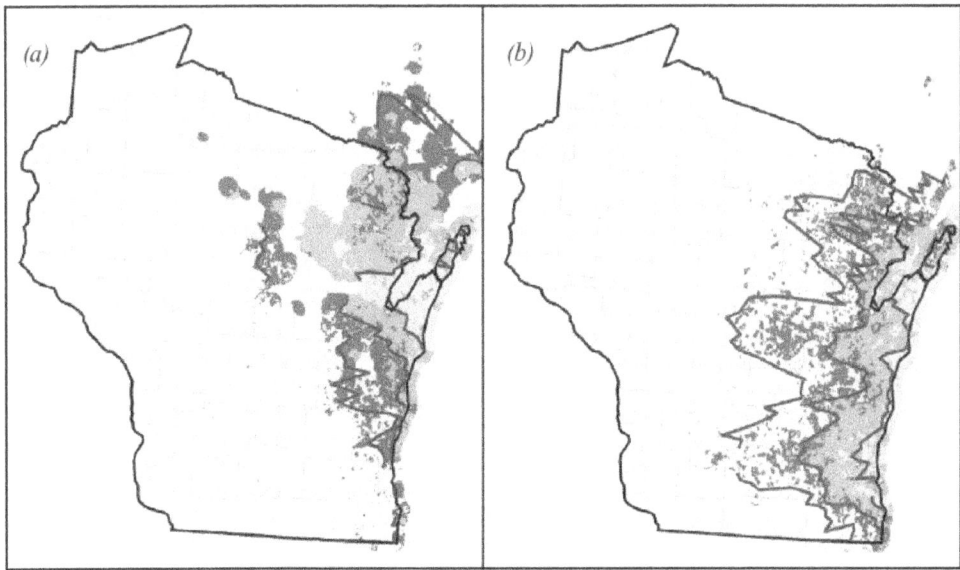

Figure 2.10.—*Interpolated moth trap-capture surfaces from Wisconsin in (a) 1995 and (b) 1996.*

several "fingers" of elevated trap capture in areas of Wisconsin, where there were no populations previously. There probably are several possible causes for these patterns; one explanation is that large numbers of males dispersed into these areas from elsewhere, e.g., outbreak populations in Michigan's lower peninsula.

Probably the most definitive piece of evidence for adult male dispersal are historical unpublished records of trap capture in the Upper Peninsula of Michigan in 1993. These records showed two major peaks of trap capture during a single season. The first peak, apparently composed of immigrant moths, was observed from July 22 to August 6, and coincided with the timing of adult development to the south, i.e., the lower peninsula. A second and much smaller peak caused by resident moths was observed from August 18 to September 9, and coincided with the timing of adult emergence in the Upper Peninsula. Positive trap captures over large, continuous areas where none were previously detected have been observed elsewhere along the expanding population front, for example North Carolina in the early 1990's, along the Ohio/Indiana border in 1998, and in central Ohio in 1999. Unfortunately little is known about the behavior of adult males or meteorological conditions that might explain why these events occur in certain locations in specific years.

Since males alone are not capable of reproducing, a cursory interpretation of these dispersal events is that they have no consequence to gypsy moth spread. However, as stated earlier, most isolated gypsy moth populations in the transition area go extinct with no intervention, and the most likely cause is an Allee effect due to a failure to find mates. However, dispersal of large numbers of males into the transition area could greatly alter this phenomenon. Dispersing males would mate with females and the result would be the persistence of a much larger proportion of isolated colonies, leading to a much higher rate of spread than would exist without male dispersal. However, it remains unclear whether the higher rates of spread observed in Wisconsin, where dispersal episodes appear to have been numerous, could be explained by this effect.

Nevertheless, Whitmire and Tobin (2006) reported that the persistence of isolated populations was much greater in Wisconsin than elsewhere in the transition area and that this elevated persistence can be expected to result in higher spread rates. They also reported that after controlling for population density, persistence was much greater among isolated populations near the continuously infested areas than among more distantly located populations. Presumably, male availability could be expected to be greater for the proximal populations and this could explain their increased persistence.

Since the spread of any invading population is the result of population growth coupled with dispersal, one could expect that any habitat characteristic that causes increases in dispersal or population growth would lead to elevated rates of spread. But despite this intuitively obvious connection between habitat quality and range expansion, there is little evidence of a strong interaction between characteristics of the habitat and spread rates. For example, in figure 1 from Liebhold et al. (1992), the expanding population front (excluding the secondary Michigan population) in 1989 was largely equidistant from the original site of introduction in Medford, Massachusetts. This indicated that historical spread had been spatially constant—except for decreased rates of spread to the north—despite considerable geographical variation in land use and forest types in the area through which the gypsy moth had expanded its range. In a more detailed analysis, Sharov et al. (1997a) examined relationships between habitat characteristics and trap capture in the central Appalachians. They found that in the uninfested area, trap captures were highest in the lower elevations, but in the transition area, trap captures were highest in the upper elevations. This suggested that these patterns may reflect higher colonization rates in low elevations (due to higher human population activity) but higher population growth at higher elevations (due to higher densities of forests).

Cold winter temperatures cause considerable mortality in overwintering gypsy moth populations. Liebhold et al. (1992) concluded that slower rates of gypsy moth spread to the north were due to this phenomenon, though the high rates of spread observed over the last 10 years in Wisconsin do not support this conclusion. Sharov et al. (1999) examined historical gypsy moth spread in Michigan and concluded that spatial and temporal variation in spread rates there were more closely associated with variation in forest composition (relative densities of gypsy moth host tree species) than with winter temperatures, though these two factors were confounded. In summary, there seems to be a weak relationship between gypsy moth spread rate and the quality of the habitat, and populations seem to be able to spread through areas of only moderate habitat quality. It may be that spread is affected both by variation in habitat invasibility for initial colonization (e.g., areas of intense human activity) and by quality for population growth, e.g., forest composition, and, therefore, no single factor alone can explain the variation in spread rates.

Conclusion

Given the enormous amount of data and intensity of research, the gypsy moth is a model system for understanding the population biology of range expansion. Spread is not a continuous expansion process as predicted by Skellam (1951). This discovery provided the basis for the implementation of the STS Program, which focuses on slowing spread by finding and eradicating isolated colonies, or suppressing their growth. The experience with gypsy moth clearly demonstrates that understanding the population biology of an invader can be instrumental in developing effective approaches to managing the invasion.

The literature is rich with information on gypsy moth range expansion, particularly the role played by the formation of colonies ahead of the infested area in gypsy moth spread. The remaining chapters of this report address various aspects of the STS Program, which was fundamentally and conceptually based on our understanding of gypsy moth invasion dynamics. The Slow the Spread approach to monitoring gypsy moth populations and collecting data, keystone aspects of the IPM philosophy, is discussed in Chapter 3.

Chapter 3. Gypsy Moth Population Monitoring and Data Collection

E. Anderson Roberts[1] and Amos H. Ziegler[2]

Introduction

The gypsy moth Slow the Spread (STS) Program is implemented along the expanding population front between generally infested and uninfested areas. In this transition zone, isolated colonies can be detected and addressed before they coalesce and contribute to further expansion of the population front. Although the geographic location of the project area is defined by the 10-moth population boundary and can change from year to year, the actual area covered by the project remains relatively constant unless new states are added (Table 3.1).

Traps baited with (+) disparlure, the synthetic gypsy moth pheromone, are used to detect and monitor low to moderate gypsy moth populations (Schwalbe 1981). STS is data intensive, entailing the placement and tending of 70,000 to 90,000 traps within the STS action and monitoring areas (Table 3.1). In addition, state sponsored surveys from non-STS areas contribute data that are incorporated into the STS database and provide information on populations outside STS. This generally brings the number of traps in the database to well over 130,000 per year. Data management occurs at the two information systems nodes in STS: at the Department of Entomology at Virginia Polytechnic Institute and State University (hereafter referred to as Virginia Tech in this report) and at the Department of Entomology at Michigan State University.

Table 3.1.—*Number of traps and area for STS Action and Monitoring Zones, 2000 to 2005*

Year	Monitoring zone		Action zone	
	Traps	Area	Traps	Area
	Number	km^2	Number	km^2
2000	7,646	143,266	61,483	218,588
2001	9,322	138,258	61,146	217,612
2002	10,027	136,096	62,204	184,854
2003	10,956	151,411	63,410	215,271
2004	10,951	175,278	65,814	215,069
2005	10,507	178,618	74,465	224,414

[1] Virginia Polytechnic Institute and State University, 315 Price Hall, Department of Entomology, Blacksburg, Virginia 24061.

[2] Michigan State University, Department of Entomology, Computational Ecology and Visualization Laboratory, 1405 South Harrison Road, 209 Manly Miles Building, East Lansing, Michigan 48824.

The STS area is divided into the action zone and the monitoring zone (Fig. 3.1). The action zone is where management strategies are applied against gypsy moth populations; the monitoring zone is where populations are surveyed to provide data used to delineate project areas, estimate population boundaries, augment data from the action zone used in the STS Decision Algorithm, and evaluate project effectiveness. No control measures are performed in the monitoring zone. Since pest management occurs in the action zone, trapping in this area is designed to detect and delimit new colonies so that intervention tactics may be applied. Thus, a higher degree of spatial resolution, achieved through a higher trap density, is required in the action zone than in the monitoring zone.

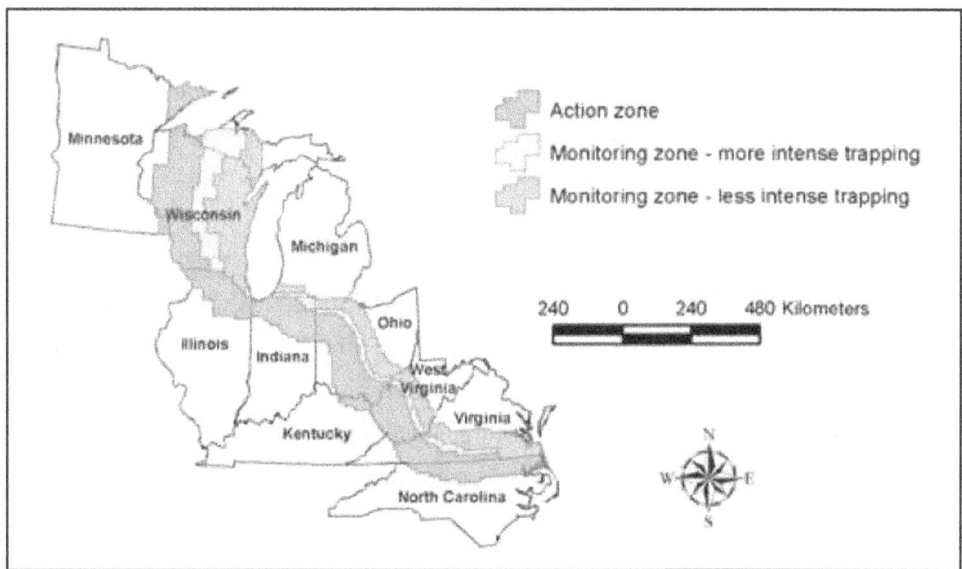

Figure 3.1.—*Location of STS Program trapping zones in 2005.*

Implementation of the Trapping Program

Each participating state is responsible for implementing and managing its trapping survey. Moreover, although the STS Program has determined a set of minimum standards with regard to trapping, each state has flexibility in meeting those standards. One example of this flexibility is in the choice of the geographic unit upon which the trapping survey is organized. In quad-based states, project boundaries and trapping surveys are organized by USGS 7.5-minute quadrangles and use metric distances between traps. This is the structure used historically in gypsy moth Integrated Pest Management (IPM) programs preceding STS (Maryland IPM, Appalachian IPM, and the STS Pilot Project). It is the default structure in STS and is used in 8 of the 10 participating states. States in the upper Midwest historically have used mile-based trapping grids in their gypsy moth programs because their land survey and road network systems are structured by county, township, and section. Within STS, Wisconsin and Illinois are county based and use a mile based grid. Project boundaries and trapping programs are structured along township (sometimes county) boundaries.

While trapping supervisors usually are permanent state employees, all states employ seasonal labor to some degree to deploy and service traps. In some states, all trapping personnel, whether permanent or seasonal, are state employees. Some states structure their survey areas into bid units which are then let out on contracts. One advantage of employing contract trappers is that it is easier to hold them to exact standards written into the contract because they do not fall under state regulations. For this reason it is important to develop tight legal contracts, which requires initial overhead from the administering state agency.

Trapping Grids

The various grid types used in STS are presented in Table 3.2. Historically, gypsy moth trapping methodologies were determined through intuition and experience coupled with available resources. Studies using data from the AIPM project and the STS Pilot Project quantified the effect of grid density on management efficacy under different spread-rate scenarios. The regular base grid of 2 km between traps (0.25 trap/km^2) currently used in STS was adequate for detecting isolated colonies (Sharov et al. 1998). The equivalent mile-based grid is 1 by 2 miles placed diagonally, yielding an intertrap distance of 2.26 km (Fig. 3.2). The monitoring zone is trapped at two densities. Sharov et al. (1997b) showed that an intertrap distance of 8 km was sufficient for estimating population boundaries and measuring the effect of project activities on the rate of spread. This is the STS standard in the part of the monitoring zone that is closest to the generally infested, or endemic, area (Fig. 3.1). However, some states trap this area more intensively

Table 3.2.—*Trapping grids employed in STS by state, 2004*

Project zones	Grid	IL	IN	KY	MI	MN	NC	OH	VA	WI	WV
Action: Base	2 mi									•	
	1X2 mi	•									
	2 km		•	•	•		•	•	•		•
	1.5 km					•					
	1 mi	•								•	
	1 km		•			•	•	•			•
Delimiting	4/mi²	•								•	
	5/mi²					•					
	500 m		•		•	•	•		•		•
	250 m		•			•		•			
	9/mi²	•								•	
	16/mi²					•					
Monitoring (proximal)	2 mi	•								•	
	3 km		•		•			•	•		•
Monitoring (distal)	3 mi	•								•	
	5 km				•			•			
	8 km								•		•

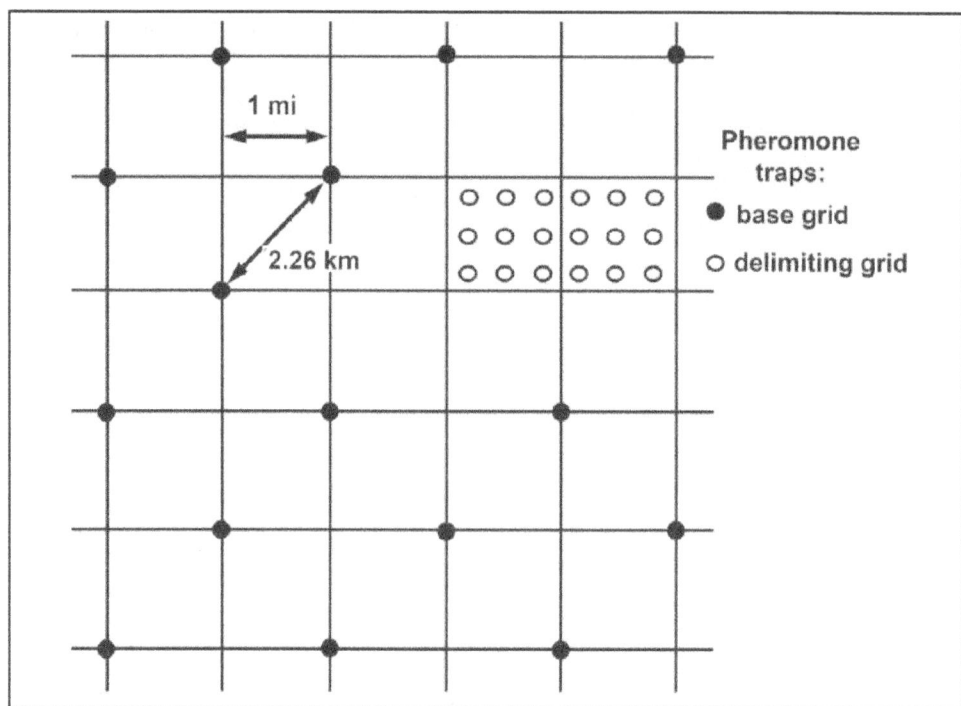

Figure 3.2.—*Trapping grid in mile-based states.*

to augment their state programs (Table 3.2). A band of variable width (usually 15 to 25 km) adjacent to the action zone is trapped at 3 km (or 2 mi). Higher resolution is needed in this area because moth counts are used in the STS Decision Algorithm to determine activities within the adjacent action zone. Deviation from these standard grids is most consistent in Wisconsin, which deploys traps in the monitoring zone at intertrap distances of 2 or 3 miles, and an intertrap distance of 1 mile in the action zone. Because of their relation to the population front and generally infested area, some states do not have gypsy moth populations sufficient to be included in the monitoring zone (Table 3.2).

Populations detected by the base grid in the action zone typically are delimited prior to treatment. The purpose of delimitation is to determine the spatial extent of the isolated population so that treatment activities can be targeted more precisely. Standard delimiting grids in STS are 500 m and 1 km in quad-based states and nine traps/mi^2 and four traps/mi^2 (intertrap distance = 536 m and 805 m, respectively) in county-based states. The choice of grid is a function of the area to be delimited, with larger areas generally delimited at 1 km or 4/mi^2. The smaller the intertrap distance, the more costly the grid in both numbers of traps per area and associated management costs. This is why there is a tendency to use coarser grids where possible, especially in large delimiting blocks. Conversely, tighter delimiting grids yield higher resolution in defining population boundaries, and treatment blocks derived from these grids are mapped more accurately to actual population levels.

Treatment blocks derived from larger spaced grids must allow for more uncertainty in population delimitation and thus may be larger than actually needed. In some cases, resources saved through implementation of coarser delimiting grids is expended in treatment costs. As we have increased the use of mating disruption (see Table 5.1), the size of treatment blocks has increased. As a result, there has been a trend toward using a coarser grid over this larger area to delineate populations for treatment. In 2004, nearly half of the 456 delimiting grids placed within the action area were 1 km or $4/mi^2$ (Table 3.3). Because coarser grids generally are applied over larger areas, this 50 percent of the count represented 85 percent of the total area delimited. The most commonly used delimiting grid remains 500 m with 44 percent of the 2004 total. However, 500-m grids generally are smaller than the coarser grids and their area in 2004 was only slightly above 13 percent (Table 3.3). States sometimes deploy delimiting grids other than those discussed, usually to increase accuracy in estimating moth density in critical areas or to more closely parallel those monitoring methods used in state or local programs.

Delimiting grids also are used to evaluate treatment efficacy (see Chapter 5). Treatments other than mating disruption can be evaluated the year of treatment. Because mating-disruption treatments saturate the affected area with pheromone, pheromone-baited traps are useless for post-treatment monitoring. These areas must be evaluated the year following treatment. Of the 456 delimiting grids placed in 2004, 196 were not for delineation of populations but used to monitor areas treated that spring with gypsy moth larvicides (109 blocks) or the previous year with mating disruption (87 blocks).

In STS there is no standard for representing delimiting grid density. In the Southern States, grids are defined by the distance between traps, e.g., 500 m, 1 km, while grids in Midwestern States are defined by the number of traps per unit area, e.g., $4/mi^2$. All states in the project had gypsy moth management programs prior to their involvement in STS. Not surprisingly, both STS and state agencies have had to accommodate one another's programs as the partnership developed. STS has been flexible in allowing states to maintain aspects of previous programs so long as those protocols complement STS standards. Conversely, states have modified long-established methodologies to better fit

Table 3.3.—*Quantity and area of delimiting grids in STS Action Zone, 2004*

Intertrap distance		Number of traps/unit area	Traps in Action Zone		Percent of area delimited
Miles	Meters		Number	Percent	
0.25	402	$16/mi^2$	5	1.1	0.2
0.6	1,000	$1/km^2$	45	9.9	49.0
0.16	250	$16/km^2$	11	2.4	0.3
0.5	805	$4/mi^2$	181	39.7	35.8
0.7	1,126	$5/mi^2$	1	0.2	< 0.1
0.3	500	$4/km^2$	202	44.3	13.3
0.3	536	$9/mi^2$	11	2.4	1.4
		Total	456	100	100

into the STS model. The seemingly inconsistent nomenclature regarding delimiting grids is an example of the overall project accommodating established state protocols.

Trap Types

Milk-carton traps can be used throughout the STS Program area because they are effective at both low and high population densities. Trappers generally prefer delta type traps because they are easier to carry and assemble, but delta traps begin to lose efficacy when they have captured about 12 moths, and become saturated at fewer than 25 moths. As a result, STS discourages the use of delta traps in areas where the moth catch might approach these numbers (Table 3.4).

Table 3.4.—*Quality assurance and quality control standards in STS Program*

Category	Standard	QA/QC checks and measures
Trap spacing	Action Zone (except WI and IL) • Delimiting grid ≈ 0.5- or 1-km spacing • Detection grid ≈ 2-km spacing Monitoring Zone (except WI and IL) • 3-km spacing in band ≈ 20 km deep adjacent to Action Zone • 8-km spacing elsewhere Action Zone (WI and IL) • Delimiting grid 9 or 4 traps/mi² • Detection grid 1 mi or 1x 2 mi Monitoring Zone (WI and IL) • 2-mi spacing in narrow band adjacent to Action Zone • 5-mi spacing elsewhere	• Grid nodes generated projectwide by GIS at master database • Grid nodes reviewed and approved by agency project managers • All traps placed using handheld GPS units or Trapper Gadget data collection devices
Integrity of the trapping grids	• 100% of grid nodes accounted for in database as deployed or omitted • 90% of grid nodes associated with deployed trap; adjacent omits avoided	• Omitted sites approved by agency managers • Web-based, real-time database reports • 10% of trap sites field checked for accuracy • Annual database summary
Trap location	• 90% of deployed traps placed within defined distance of grid node (± 30% of intertrap distance)	• Positional data collected using GPS units as data recorders • Database validation routines, reports • 10% of trap sites field checked for accuracy
Trap style	Action Zone • Milk-carton traps can be used in detection or delimit grids • Delta traps can be used only in detection grid or in delimit grids when moth capture in previous year < 5 • Milk-carton traps can be used in detection or delimit grids Monitoring Zone • Milk-carton traps used throughout	• Database validation routines, error reports • 10% of trap sites field checked for accuracy

Table 3.4.—*Quality assurance and quality control standards in STS Program (continued)*

Category	Standard	QA/QC checks and measures
Trap placement and removal schedules	• Schedules for completion of trap deployment and initiation of trap removal based on phenology • Target dates set for zones of similar elevation and latitude using best available local knowledge	• Zone map based on weather, elevation, and latitude used to run phenology model (GMPHEN and BioSIM) • Database runs phenology model with current-year weather data to check for areas where trap set and removal out of sync with phenology; results documented in annual report
Personnel skills	• Implementing agencies document procedures used to ensure that individuals collecting and processing data have demonstrated qualifications	Certification of annual training provided to field personnel covering: • Use of GPS and other field equipment • Trap assembly and moth identification • Map reading and field navigation • Safety and public relations • Trapping manuals that address protocols for data collection and processing • Safety action plans include methods for addressing identified hazards

Alternate Life Stages

Although gypsy moth managers in the generally infested area typically rely on egg-mass surveys as part of management programs aimed at suppressing outbreak and defoliating gypsy moth populations, monitoring for life stages other than male moths is not a part of the STS Program. Egg-mass surveys are resource intensive and not feasible for the large STS area, and populations are sufficiently low as to make such surveys generally ineffective. That being said, some states select high-catch areas for egg-mass sampling, and, managers occasionally find an area within STS where other life stages are evident. While the STS Decision Algorithm has no mechanism for factoring this information into its analysis, it is presented informally during the planning process where it may have an impact on recommendations for treatment or delimiting.

Data Collection

In STS, all trap sites to be addressed during the survey season are determined *a priori* based on the analysis of the previous year's data. Trapping data from the previous season are processed through the Decision Algorithm (Chapters 4 and 5, Tobin et al. 2004), and the results are reviewed and edited by Federal and state cooperators. The products of these meetings are the delineation of STS action and monitoring areas and associated trapping grids as well as proposed treatment blocks throughout the entire STS area. Usually, areas trapped under state programs also are defined at this time. Throughout this series of "STS Roadshows," these proposed activities are incorporated in real time into the STS GIS. GIS specialists at Virginia Tech use this "project structure" data layer to assign all trapping sites for each state. Associated with each trap location are relevant data such as ID, grid type, trap type, project area, state, and agency. This information is distributed to each agency and also loaded into the STS Oracle® database where it awaits complementary trapping data from the field survey. In addition, personnel at Michigan State University information systems node use these intended trap locations to create, print, laminate, and distribute trapping survey maps (Fig. 6.5).

Trapper training and the beginning of trap placement occur from early April (Southern States) through early June (Northern States). Trap removal is completed by late September in the South but continues into October or November in the North. A critical trapping issue is to have all traps in the field for the duration of male moth flight, which is long over such a large and varied project area. Trap placement and removal currently are guided by a modified version of the gypsy moth phenology model GMPHEN (Sheehan 1992) implemented using BioSIM software (Régnière and Sharov 1998). Using 30-year average temperature data, the authors derived dates of 5- and 95-percent emergence from the date of peak flight. As applied in STS and to account for annual variation, 5 days were subtracted from the 5-percent emergence date and were added to the 95-percent emergence date. These dates currently range from the end of May for trap placement through the middle of October for removal. Management constraints often preclude strict adherence to the dates suggested by the phenology model, and managers often use experiential data accumulated within each state to adjust model recommendations. Currently, the model suggests trapping guidelines as well as a quality control assessment with respect to whether a trap-catch value might be suspect because of the timing of trap placement or removal.

The number of traps assigned to a trapper varies across the project and is a function of topography and the structure of road networks. Across the project, fulltime trappers assume responsibility for as few as 200 traps to as many as 700. Trappers in difficult terrain, e.g., mountainous, swampy, or densely vegetated areas, require more time to reach the intended site. Each intended trap location is the center of a circle with a radius equal to 30 percent of the intertrap distance (Fig. 3.3). A trapper may place a trap anywhere within this "target circle." The target circle facilitates trap placement while maintaining the integrity of the trapping grid. As the intertrap distance decreases, as in delimiting grids, the size of the target circle also decreases, reducing the available area for trap placement and thus increasing the time required to place and service traps. In many areas, trappers remain near their vehicles to place and service traps whereas other areas require significant effort to reach intended sites. Traps are visited at least twice—for placement and removal—but most traps also are inspected during midseason.

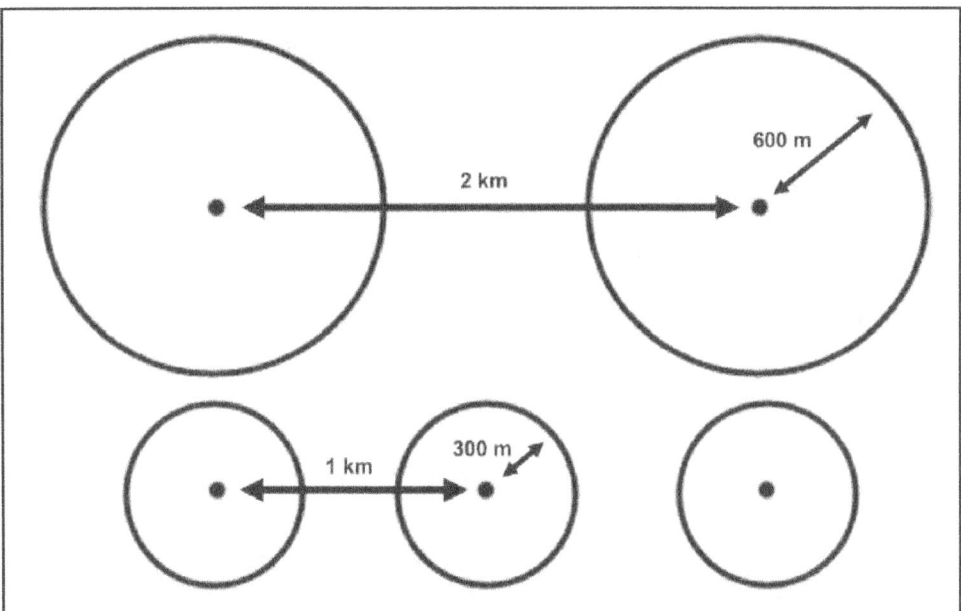

Figure 3.3.—*Pheromone trap-grid node and associated target circle.*

Trappers use recreational grade global positioning system (GPS) receivers to record trapping data during trap placement and inspection (Fig. 3.4). Most trappers navigate using trapping maps, usually USGS 7.5-minute quadrangles or a version of a county map. These can be created digitally or developed within each state using available paper maps. In some states, trappers load trap locations into the GPS receiver using customized interface software developed by the project (GPSi) and then use the receiver to navigate to the trap. By front-loading the database with a large amount of information associated with the trap locations, we have minimized data-collection requirements during trap services. At placement, trappers need enter only the unique site identification number and trap type. At inspection, trappers record unique site identification numbers, whether the visit is a midseason or final inspection, trap condition, and moth catch. Trappers may omit a trap under certain conditions, such as the presence of a safety hazard, when the site is inaccessible, or when a landowner denies access. In this instance, the trap-placement record must contain the reason for the omitted information; typically, omitted sites must be approved by the trapper's supervisor.

The integrity of the STS Program is maintained by adhering to a specific set of established standards (Table 3.4) that address projectwide issues such as trap-grid spacing and integrity, trap types, and timing of trap placement and removal. It is these standards that states must adhere to regardless of how their monitoring program is structured.

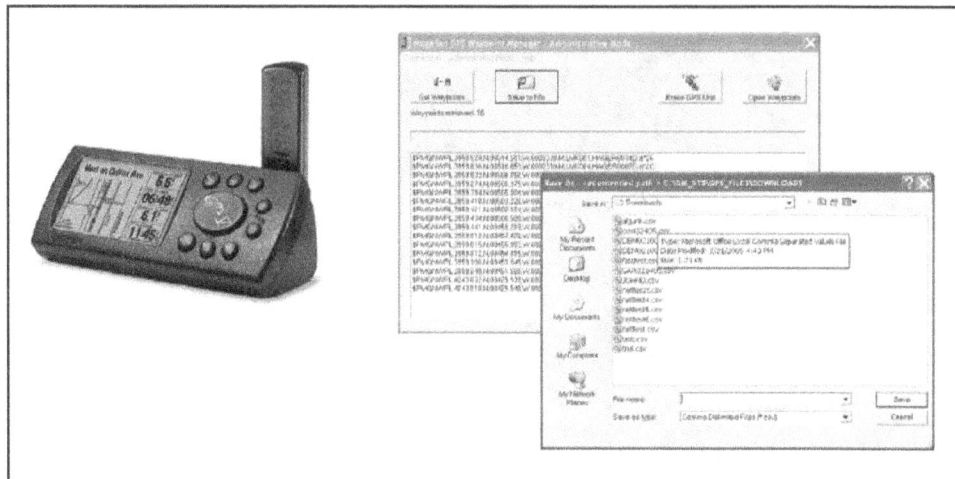

Figure 3.4.—*Garmin V GPS unit and GPSi software.*

The Trapper Gadget

During the 2002-05 field seasons, a limited number of prototype data-collection devices were used to test the feasibility of constructing a more intelligent GPS unit. The Trapper Gadget is a Windows Mobile-based (formerly known as PocketPC) PDA with an integrated GPS receiver (Fig. 3.5). The device hosts a region-specific subset of the STS database and provides a highly customized user interface for collection and manipulation of geocentric STS data. Custom software was written to specifically address STS trapping protocols. The device uses its GPS receiver to determine the location and nearest trap site. It then leads the trapper through the data-collection process so as to remove the possibility of data entry errors. The units continue to be used with success in Kentucky,

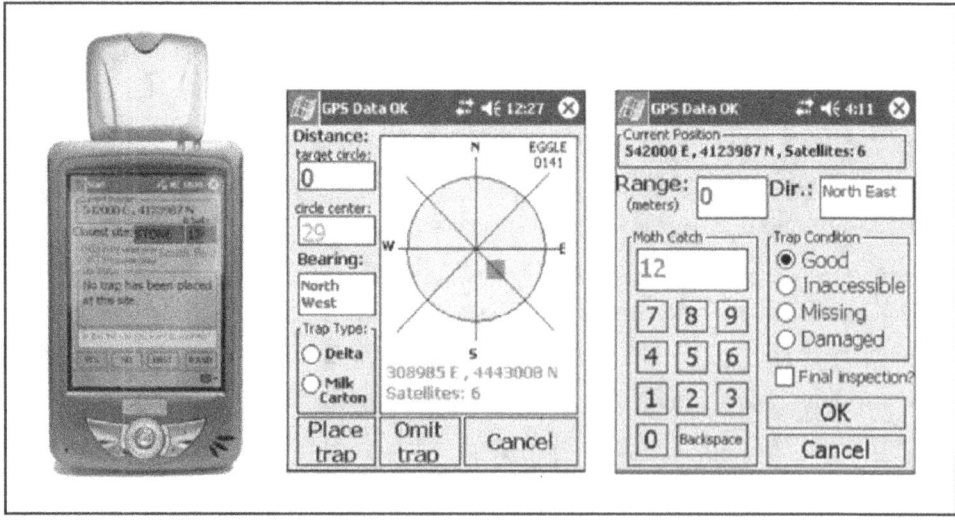

Figure 3.5.—*STS Trapper Gadget and example software screens.*

Illinois, and Indiana and were tested in 2005 in Minnesota, West Virginia, and Michigan. Current Trapper Gadget hardware is not sufficiently robust to withstand the rigors of some trapping areas, and it works best for those trappers who can leave the units in their vehicle.

The Trapper Gadget system consists of the GPS/PDA collection device, a suite of desktop tools that reside on the supervisor's computer, and access via the STS Database Portal (http://www.gmsts.org/operations/) to the trapping database for which a particular Gadget will be responsible.

Quality Control Checks

In accordance with STS standards (Table 3.4), states are required to monitor at least 10 percent of their sites for quality control. These inspections, performed by supervisors, assess trapping performance and identify trappers who need assistance; the mechanics of trapping are emphasized. A trap might fail the inspection if it is assembled or set improperly, labeled incorrectly, or if a trapper's records are incomplete.

Data Flow

The general data flow within STS from trappers through the STS database, GIS, and Decision Algorithm is shown in Figure 3.6. In most states, trappers meet with their supervisors once a week to download data from their GPS receiver or Trapper Gadget using custom STS-specific software: the GPS Interface (GPSi) for commercial GPS receivers or the Gadget Desktop Utilities for Trapper Gadget collection devices. The use of STS-specific software illustrates one of the tenets of information management in STS: where possible, STS has developed specific software tools that address STS needs and eliminate problems often encountered with proprietary commercial software. All STS software tools are available as self-installing packages that can be managed easily by cooperators.

Once downloaded from the GPS receiver, supervisors can load the data directly into TrapView, another STS tool for display and error-checking (Figs. 3.6 and 3.7). TrapView is a simple GIS viewer that displays GPS data along with the intended site information or other data themes (Fig. 3.7). It checks for and flags simple errors and provides an interface for correcting and saving the GPS file. Written in MapObjects from Environmental Systems Research Institute, TrapView is a stand-alone program and requires no supporting software. Supervisors save original or edited GPS files in a standardized directory structure and then use the STS GPS File Uploader to transfer files through FTP (File Transfer Protocol) to the proper directory on the appropriate database server. The five Southern States in STS submit trapping data to Virginia Tech while the Northern States submit data to Michigan State University. The STS Oracle® database has stringent file-format requirements and it is critical that GPS files are complete and properly formatted.

The GPS File Uploader is a simple interface that allows users to select GPS files to transfer and perform file-formatting checks in the process. Files failing the format test remain on the supervisor's desktop computer for further attention. At each database node, an automated program monitors the FTP server target directory for each state's GPS files. Every 10 minutes, the STS Database Autoloader collects new GPS files from the server and submits them to the database. Following the completion of the Autoloader job, automatic email notification is sent informing the cooperator of the success or failure of the GPS file loadings.

Automating the data flow has reduced the number of errors arriving at the database and has significantly reduced the amount of time before cooperators can access their data. Upon insertion into the Oracle® database, survey data are reconciled with proposed trap-site information through a final set of validations, records with errors are managed in separate database tables from the error-free data. Most trapper errors are the result of typographical errors at data entry or of the trapper mistakenly believing he or she is at a location different from where he or she actually is. Errors generated within the database are available for correction through the STS Operations Portal. State representatives may log in, correct errors, and create reports in real time. STS trapping data, from GPS receiver to Oracle® database (including error reporting and correction), can be processed in minutes. Once in the database trapping data are accessible by other components of the STS Information System. These include the GIS at both Virginia Tech and Michigan State University as well as the STS Decision Algorithm (see Chapters 4 and 5) housed at Virginia Tech.

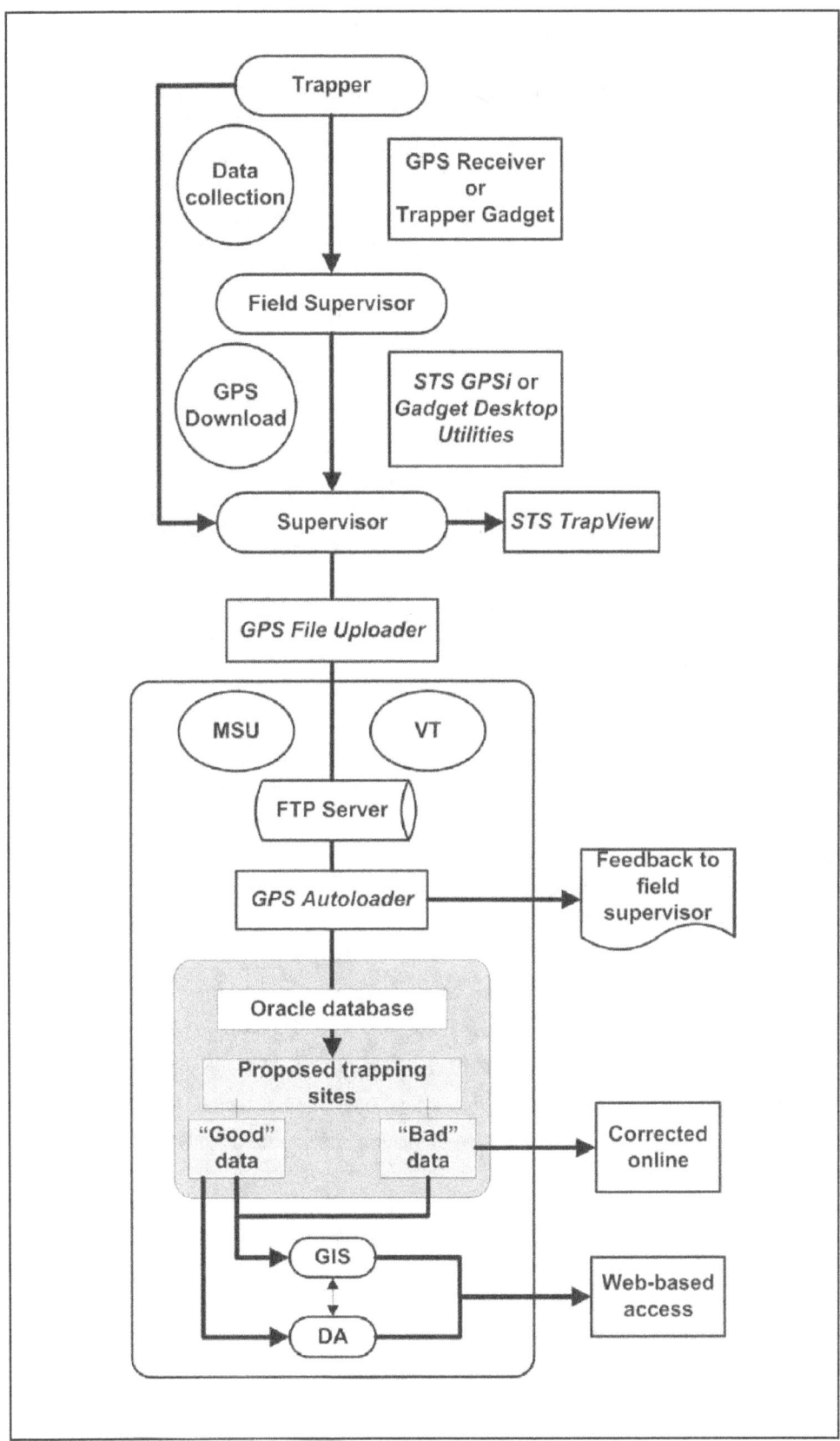

Figure 3.6.—*General data flow of the STS Program.*

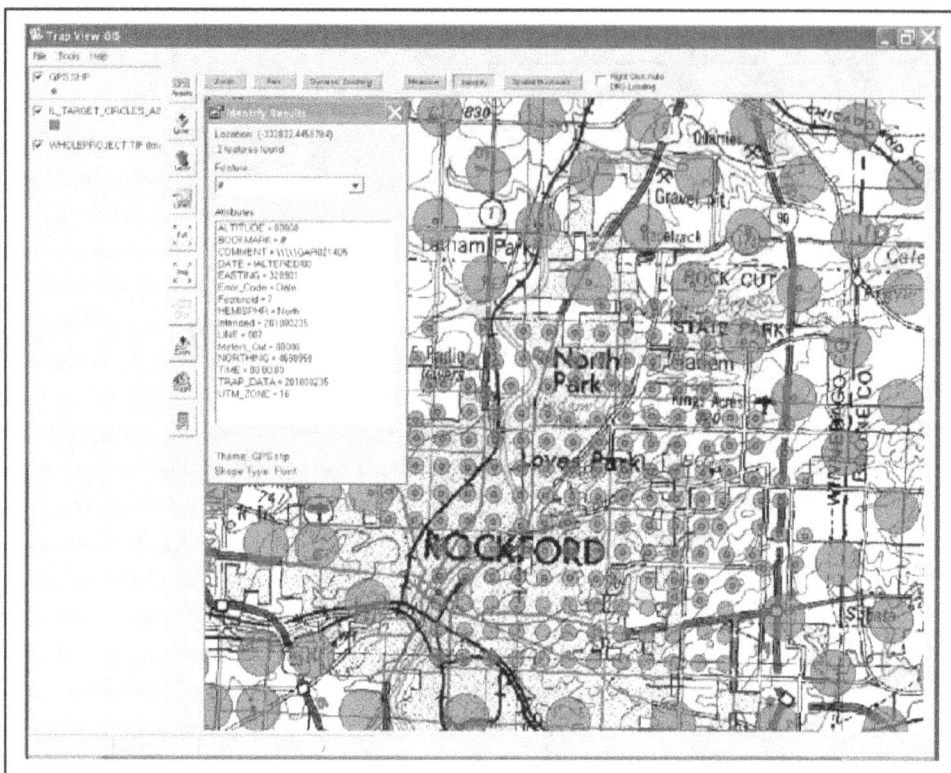

Figure 3.7.—*TrapView screen capture showing downloaded GPS locations (red dots) with target circles of intended trap locations.*

Conclusion

The successful implementation of the STS methodology is dependent on intensive monitoring of low-level gypsy moth populations. The project has developed a set of sound sampling procedures that optimize trapping resources, maintain data integrity through established quality control protocols, and allows cooperating states flexibility in adapting STS to their established gypsy moth programs. The trapping program is enhanced through the use of advanced data collection and GPS file-management tools coupled to software written specifically for STS operations. Chapters 4 and 5 describe the Decision Algorithm used in Slow the Spread to analyze these data.

Chapter 4. The Decision Algorithm: Selection of and Recommendation for Potential Problem Areas

Patrick C. Tobin[1] and Alexei A. Sharov[2]

Introduction

The Slow the Spread (STS) Program focuses on populations in the transition zone that are not targeted by traditional eradication and suppression efforts. In this zone, most areas are devoid of gypsy moth populations, and any populations present are newly established or establishing, generally at low abundance, and discontinuous from one another. The trapping of male moths through pheromone-baited traps is the primary method of sampling because other life stages are difficult to find. The strategy in STS is to use grids of pheromone-baited traps to locate and delimit isolated populations. Once these populations have been delimited, attempts are made to eradicate these populations or suppress their growth to prevent them from contributing to the progression of the population front. The Decision Algorithm is a critical component in this process. In this chapter we describe the principles and general methodology of the Decision Algorithm, and it is largely based on two previously published papers (Sharov et al. 2002b, Tobin et al. 2004).

The Decision Algorithm

The conceptual design of the Decision Algorithm dates back to the Appalachian Integrated Pest Management Demonstration Project (see Fig. 1.3), which was implemented in central West Virginia and Virginia from 1988 to 1992 (Fig. 4.1, Ravlin et al. 1992). During the STS Pilot Project, management decisions followed this conceptual framework but decisions were made largely by visual interpretation of trap-grid data. Originally written in the C programming language, the Decision Algorithm was developed to automate this process and is based on the optimization of intervention action in a model of gypsy moth spread (Sharov et al. 1998b). Data from pheromone-baited traps are used in the Decision Algorithm to objectively locate isolated gypsy moth populations or "Potential Problem Areas" (PPAs). These PPAs are then evaluated to recommend a course of action, which can include treatment, more intensive monitoring to delimit the extent of the population, or doing nothing (Fig. 4.2).

---

[1] USDA Forest Service, Northern Research Station, 180 Canfield Street, Morgantown, West Virginia 26505.
[2] Laboratory of Genetics, National Institute on Aging (NIA/NIH), 333 Cassell Drive, Suite 3000, Baltimore, Maryland 21224.

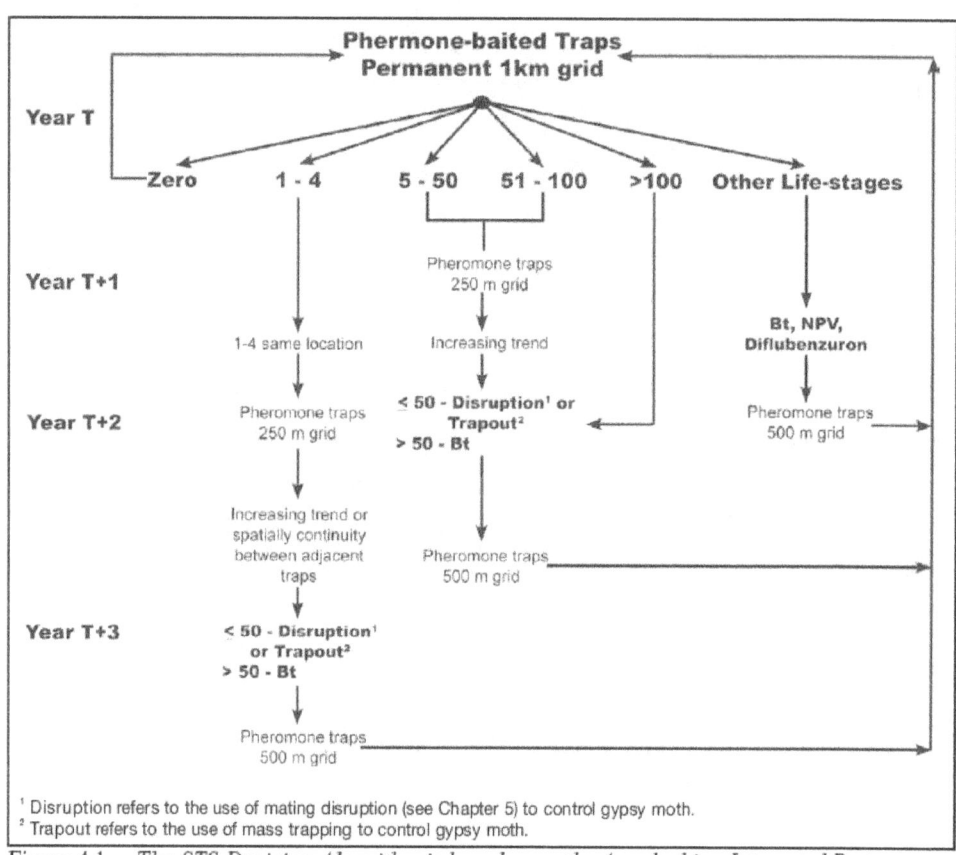

Figure 4.1.—*The STS Decision Algorithm is based upon the Appalachian Integrated Pest Management demonstration project (from Figure 2 in Ravlin et al. 1992).*

Selection of Potential Problem Areas

The Decision Algorithm uses three methods to select PPAs. The STS transition zone, which currently encompasses an area of about 344,000 km², is partitioned into a series of 40- by 40-km regions. Within each region, the Decision Algorithm analyzes trap-catch data and generates an empirical distribution of moth counts within these regions. Trap locations or areas within each region that are in the upper percentiles of the distribution represent the locations or areas with the highest moth counts in the 40- by 40-km region.

The three methods used by Decision Algorithm aim to determine trap locations or areas that have recorded elevated counts of male moths. The first method is described in Figure 4.3. In this method, trap locations for which the moth count exceeds the 98th percentile within each 40- by 40-km region are identified. The other two methods use smoothed interpolated surfaces (on a 1-km grid) that are derived from trap-catch data, and spatial interpolations that are based on median indicator kriging (Isaaks and Srivastava 1989). The second method uses kriged values to locate areas where interpolated values exceeded the 92nd percentile of the distribution. The third method is an extension of the previous method in which interpolated values from the previous and current year

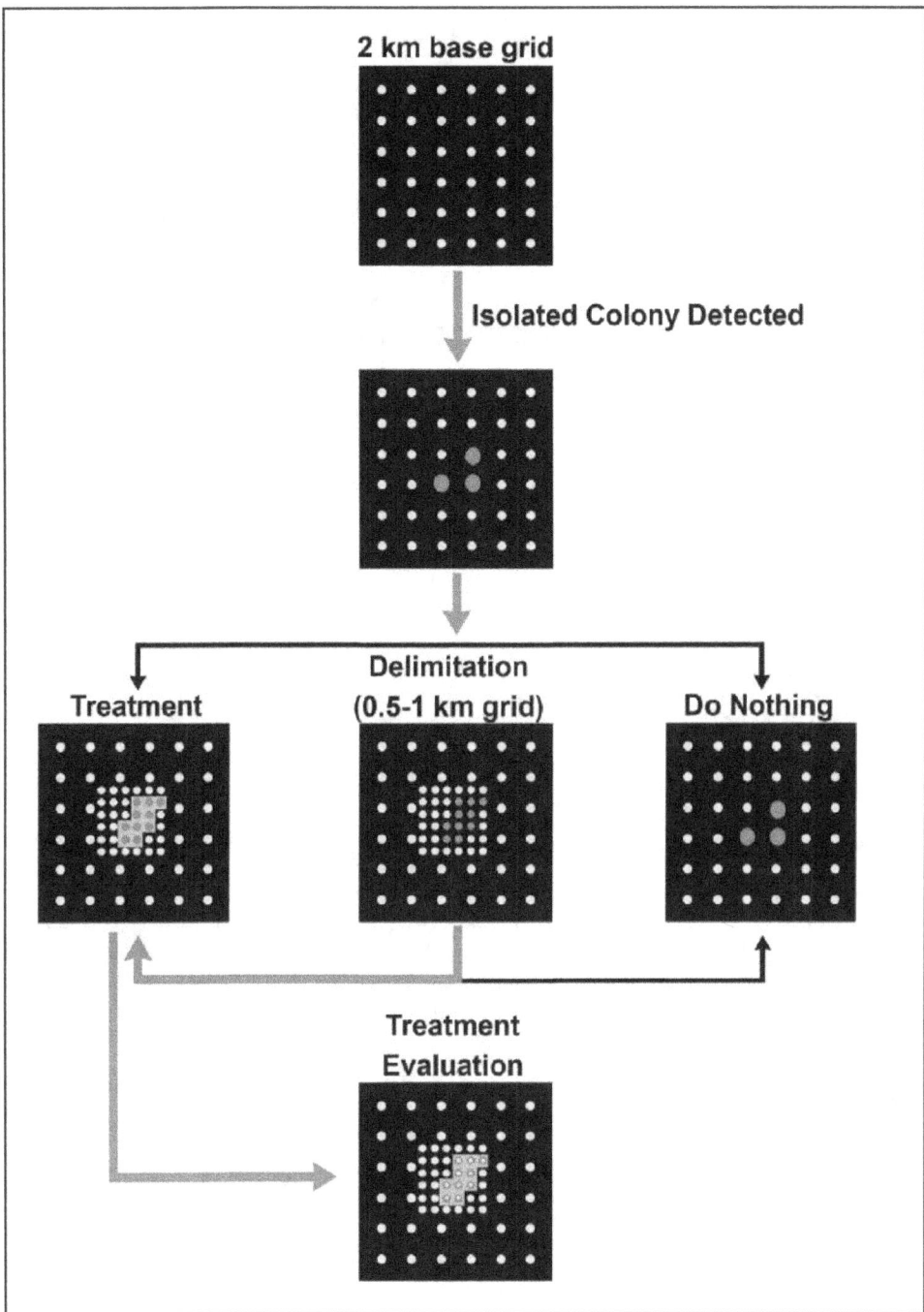

Figure 4.2.—*Simplified flow chart of the STS strategy process. Red arrows show the most likely route when an isolated colony is detected. Upon detection, the area around the colony is delimited the following year to more precisely outline the infestation before treatment (modified from Figure 3 in Tobin et al. 2004).*

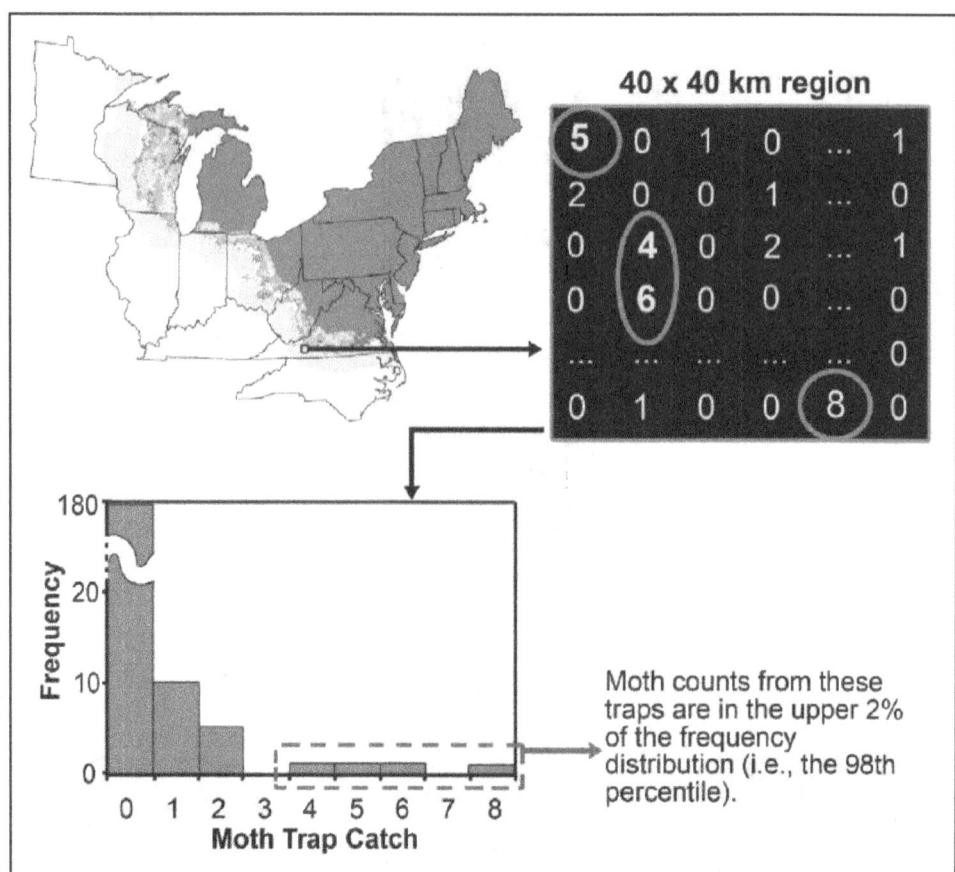

Figure 4.3.—*The Decision Algorithm uses three independent methods to select Potential Problem Areas (PPAs). One method selects locations at which moth counts, within a 40- by 40-km subregion of the Action Zone (gray area), are in the 98th percentile of the empirical frequency distribution. The other two methods also use a 40- by 40-km subregion but select PPAs from an interpolated surface based on moth counts. One selects interpolated areas that are in the 92nd percentile; the other selects interpolated areas in the 92nd percentile when the previous and current years are considered.*

are considered. By overlaying trap-catch data from two years, the Decision Algorithm may be able to detect isolated areas through their temporal persistence even though they may not be sufficiently spatially distinct to detect data used from only a single year. In this method, we may be able to detect PPAs that are difficult to identify from one year's data, due to intensive male moth dispersal in a particular year. Kriged values are used in both years and the product of kriged values for each 1-km grid cell is calculated. Areas where the product exceeds the 92nd percentile of the distribution of products are then selected.

These three methods are used collectively and independently so that results from all three methods are considered jointly and equally in the selection process. The threshold percentiles used by the Decision Algorithm, i.e., 98th and 92nd, were chosen because they generally reflected locations that were determined to be indicative of PPAs that were actually managed. Because each method relies on the empirical distribution of moth counts over a 40- by 40-km region, it is possible to identify as a PPA a trap for which the moth count was 1 if all the other traps in the region caught no moths. Therefore, the next step in the Decision Algorithm is to assign a priority to each PPA and make objective recommendations for each PPA that optimize the effort to manage the gypsy moth over a large regional scale with a finite set of resources.

Assigning a Course of Action to Potential Problem Areas

The number of PPAs identified in each year vary (Table 4.1). The Decision Algorithm calculates two indices, a **delimiting index** and a **priority index**, for each PPA to assist in objectively assigning an appropriate action. Although the next two sections will address these indices, additional technical details on the calculation of the delimiting and priority indices can be found in Tobin et al. (2004) and on the STS Decision Support Web site maintained by Virginia Tech (http://da.ento.vt.edu/).

Table 4.1.—*Potential Problems Areas detected under STS Project, 1999-2005*

Year	Number of Potential Problem Areas
1999	767
2000	755
2001	764
2002	640
2003	945
2004	818
2005	740

Delimiting Index

The delimiting index is used as a guide to indicate the need for more intensive monitoring to delineate the extent of the infestation before treatment. The delimiting index, D, is a function of trap density per square km (K) and the area of the PPA (A),

$$D = K \times Z(A) . \tag{4.1}$$

In PPAs that have an area of at least 9 km², trap density, K, can be estimated simply as the number of traps in the PPA divided by its area. However, for smaller PPAs, often there are too few traps with which to adequately estimate a trap density. For these PPAs, trap density is calculated by including traps that are within 3 km of the PPA.

The function $Z(A)$ is an adjustment coefficient that depends on the area of the PPA. The reason behind this adjustment is that smaller PPAs require a higher trap density for delimiting than larger PPAs because of the difference in spatial resolution. In these small

PPAs, a 0.5-km trapping grid generally is used to delineate the extent of the gypsy moth population. In larger PPAs, a 0.5-km trapping grid is not feasible; instead, we generally use a 1.0-km trapping grid, which results in sufficient trap density for the PPA due to the increased number of total traps. We use the following function for $Z(A)$

$$Z(A) = 4 - 3\exp\left[\frac{-(A-1)^2}{900}\right]. \tag{4.2}$$

In small PPAs, $Z(A)$ is approximately 1 so that $D \approx K$. However, in larger colonies, $Z(A)$ approaches 4 so that D is approximately equal to a quadruple trap density in larger PPAs to compensate for decrease in trap density. The reason behind equation 4.2 is that a high trap density, such as a 0.5-km trapping grid, is not needed in large PPAs. Instead, a 1-km trapping grid can be used in large PPAs; this fourfold decrease in trap density is compensated by the multiplier $Z(A)$.

Priority Index

The priority index, P, is the most complex aspect of the STS Decision Algorithm. The number of PPAs identified by the Decision Algorithm in a given year can be fairly high (Table 4.1) and consequently include more areas than can be managed. The priority index is an important criterion that places a higher priority on PPAs that, based on the biology and ecology of the dynamics of gypsy moth spread, have the greatest potential to contribute to the spread of the insect. Thus, it ranks the overall importance of each PPA so that the more critical PPAs can be targeted first given the constraints on available STS resources. The priority index comprises four primary components:

$$P = F1 + F2 + F3 + F4, \tag{4.3}$$

each of which represents a different aspect in assigning the priority to each PPA (Table 4.2).

The function $F1$ represents the persistence of the PPA and is a function of the maximum moth counts in the PPA in the current year ($Nmax_t$) and previous year ($N'max_{t-1}$). Note that there is a primed designation for the maximum moth count in the previous year because in certain cases, some PPAs are small, i.e., < 9 km^2, and might have few or no traps from the previous year. In this case, we consider trap-catch data from locations within 3 km of the PPA when determining the maximum moth count for the previous year. Recall that this is similar to the manner in which trap density, used in the Delimiting Index, is estimated in smaller PPAs (see section on the Delimiting Index). The function F1 is calculated according to

$$F1 = \log_e [Nmax_t + 0.5Nmax_t (\min(Nmax_t, N'max_{t-1}) +1) +1] . \tag{4.4}$$

Table 4.2.—*General roles and effects of four primary components to Decision Algorithm Priority Index*

Function	General Role	Effect
F1	Considers population density in PPA in current and previous year	Higher population density produces higher Priority Index
F2	Considers distance of PPA from generally infested areas	PPAs within 15 km of beginning of Action Area (boundary closest to generally infested area) have a lower Priority Index
F3	Considers population density in background populations adjacent to PPA	Lower density in background population produces higher Priority Index
F4	Considers effects of other nearby PPAs on PPA being evaluated	PPAs behind other PPAs have a lower Priority Index

The $(\min(Nmax_t, N'max_{t-1})$ component of equation 4.4 selects the smaller maximum moth count between the current and previous year. In this function, PPAs with a previous history of a high moth count are assigned higher priority index values relative to those in which the maximum moth count was lower without applying a penalty to PPAs for which the counts increased from few to no moths to high moth counts (Fig. 4.4).

The second component of the priority index considers the Euclidean distance, d, between the PPA and beginning of the STS action zone, which is adjacent to the leading edge of the gypsy moth population front. It is calculated according to

$$F2 = \min (0.002d, 0.222d - 3.3) . \tag{4.5}$$

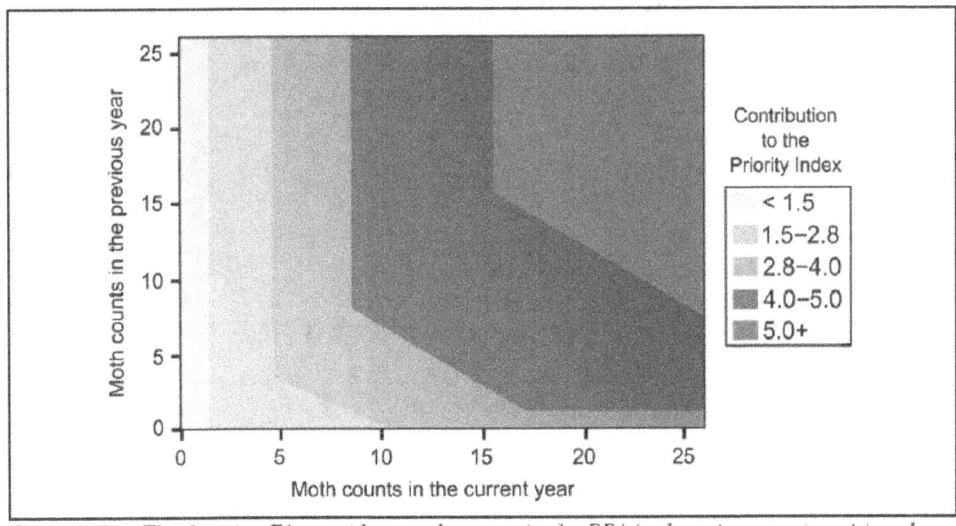

Figure 4.4.—*The function* F1 *considers moth counts in the PPA in the prior year (y-axis) and current year (x-axis) when calculating its contribution to the Priority Index. PPAs where moth counts have been high for consecutive years or PPAs with moth counts that are increasing from year to year are given higher priority.*

This is a piece-linear function that is negative when d is small and slightly positive when d is large, that is, the priority of a PPA is decreased when it is closer to the population front. Specifically, a substantially lower priority is given to PPAs within 15 km of the beginning of the action zone (Fig. 4.5). This component is based on the historical rate of gypsy moth spread, which was estimated as about 20 km/yr (Liebhold et al. 1992; Sharov et al. 1997b, 1999; Tobin et al. 2007). On the basis of this historical assessment, STS formulated a target spread rate of 10 km/yr, or a reduction of 50 percent. A threshold of 15 km in $F2$ was a compromise between historical and expected rates of spread, assuming that any PPAs within 15 km of the population front would soon be within the generally infested zone. Therefore, the impact of any management tactics for these PPAs likely would be too ephemeral to be economically viable.

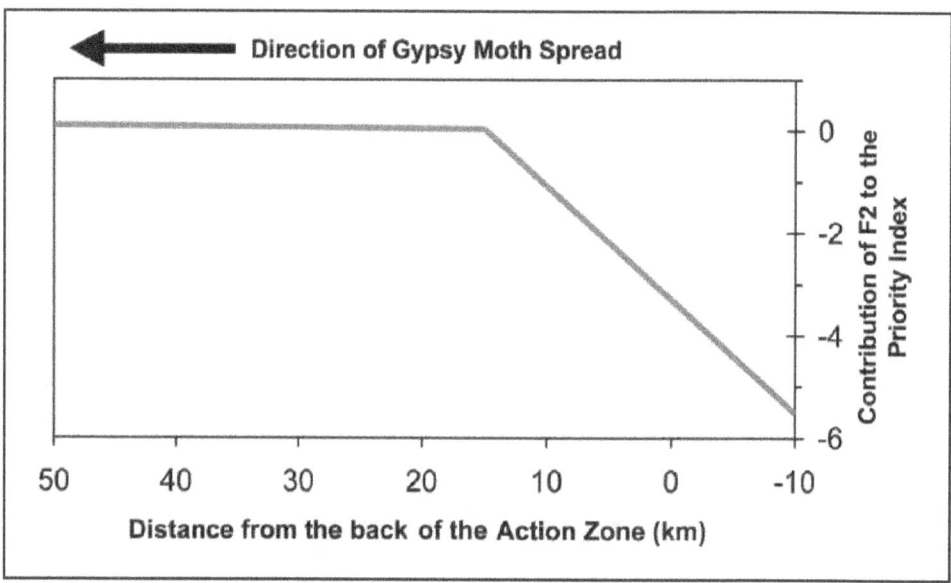

Figure 4.5.—*Contribution of F2 to the Priority Index (modified from Figure 5 in Tobin et al. 2004). This component considers the distance between the PPA and the beginning of the Action Zone, and places a substantial penalty on PPAs closer to the population front.*

The third component, $F3$, is a linear function that considers the neighboring background populations around the PPA in the current (Nb_t) and previous year (Nb_{t-1}),

$$F3 = 0.5\ Nb_{t-1} - 1.3\ Nb_t. \qquad (4.6)$$

The background population is defined by moth counts from pheromone-baited traps located within 25 km from the center of the PPA; data from traps within the PPA are excluded. This component reduces the priority of a PPA if the background moth abundance is high (Fig. 4.6). For example, this component would reduce the priority of such PPAs in years characterized by intensive moth dispersal. However, the background moth abundance from the previous year also could increase the priority of the PPA when, for example, male moth dispersal has decreased in the current year, causing a decrease in background moth abundance. In such a case, the priority of the PPA is increased.

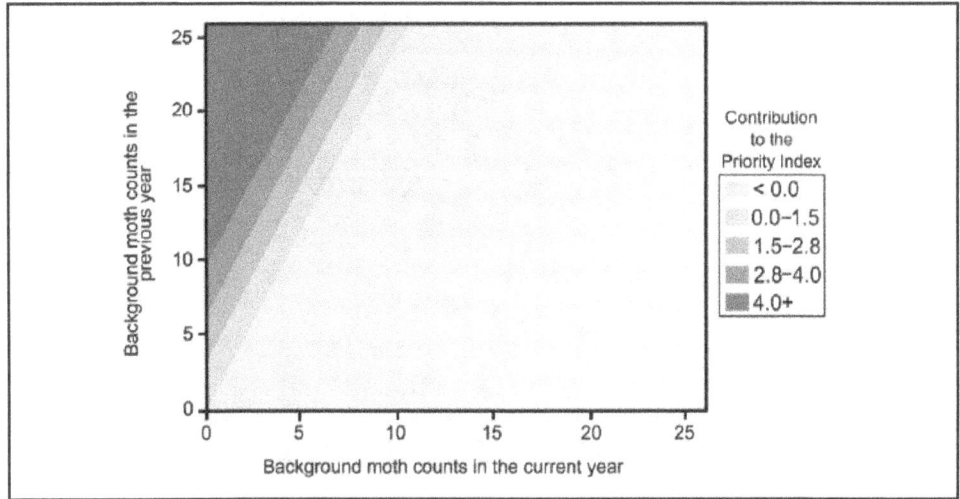

Figure 4.6.—*The function* F3 *considers the change in moth counts in nearby, background populations around the PPA in the prior (y-axis) and current year (x-axis) when calculating its contribution to the Priority Index. If background populations are declining but the PPA was still selected, a spatially isolated colony has been identified for management under STS. When the background populations increase, this potentially highlights a problem in identifying the spatial extent of the PPA.*

The last component of the priority index is the most complex and considers the influence PPAs have on each other when assigning priority. It is calculated according to

$$F4 = -0.1 \sum_i w\left(x_i, y_i\right), \tag{4.7}$$

where x_i is the distance from a PPA of interest with respect to the i-th PPA measured in the direction perpendicular to the population front, and y_i is the distance between these PPAs in the direction parallel to the population front. The function $w(x, y)$ is

$$w(x, y) = \begin{cases} 0.5(1 - \exp(z \div 10))(\cos(3\alpha) + 1) & \text{if } |\alpha| < 60° \\ 0 & \text{otherwise} \end{cases}, \tag{4.8}$$

where z is the Euclidean distance between PPAs, and $\alpha = \tan^{-1}(y \div x)$. The equation (4.8) applies a weight to only PPAs that are within 60° of another (Fig. 4.7). The sum in equation (4.7) is then taken over all other PPAs that meet all of the following criteria: 1) they are located farther away from the population front than the PPA being evaluated, 2) they are located within the STS action zone, and 3) they have a priority index of at least 2.5. If a PPA is located in the intersection of several PPAs, its priority index is

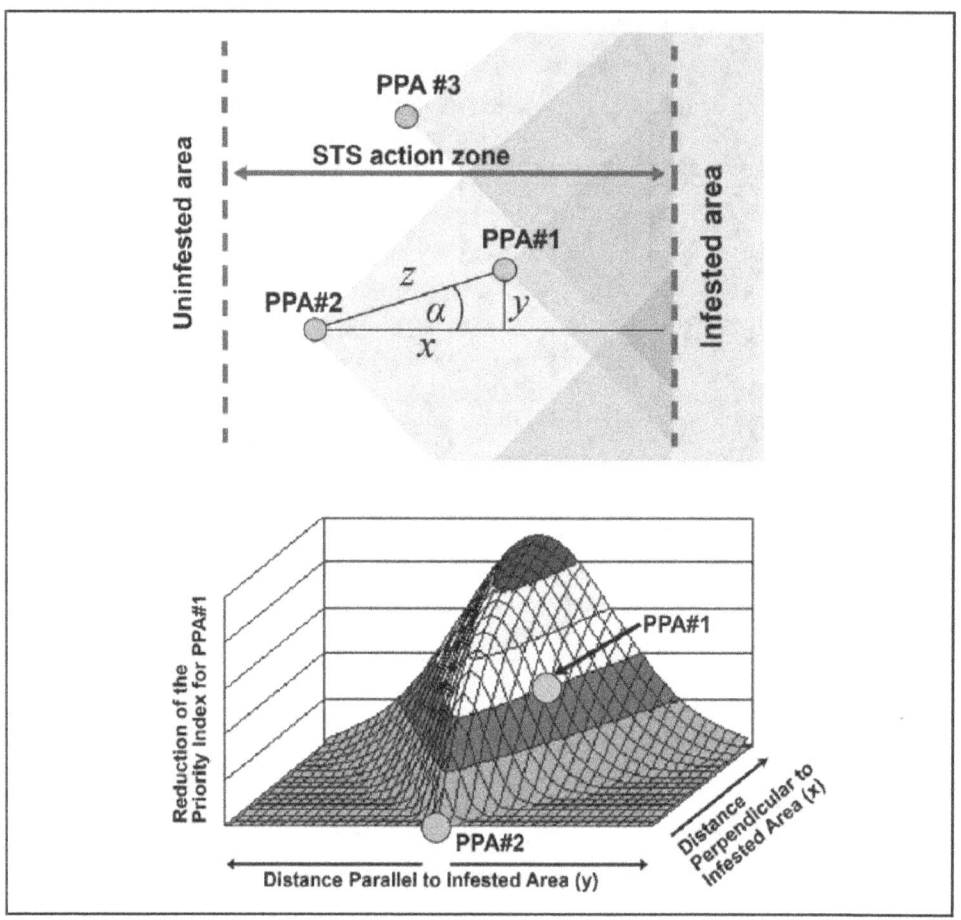

Figure 4.7.—*The shadow of influence (F4 Component) and its effect on the Priority Index: each PPA casts a "shadow" such that the distal PPAs influence the priority of other PPAs within its "wake." In certain cases, PPAs can be located in the wake of several PPAs. In this example, PPA #2 reduces the priority of PPA #1, while PPA #2 and #3 exert no influence on each other. This component places a greater priority on the more distal populations, whose establishment and growth generally contributes to higher gypsy moth spread rates. For a PPA to be in the wake of another PPA, the angle α must be $\leq 60°$.*

reduced by the sum of effects of all these PPAs. The logic here is that any PPAs located in back of (proximal to) other PPAs should have reduced priority because there is no point in addressing proximal populations if there are other populations at more distant locations (Fig. 4.7); in other words, these more distal populations have greater potential for increased spread and should receive higher priority.

Thresholds of the Delimiting and Priority Indices

Thresholds of the delimiting and priority indices for recommending a course of action were calibrated based on PPAs identified from historical trap-catch data and implemented actions for PPAs from Virginia, West Virginia, and North Carolina from the STS Pilot Project (1996 to 2000), because the actions taken in these areas reduced spread by 60 percent over historical levels (Sharov and Liebhold 1998a, Sharov et al. 2002b). The Decision Algorithm calculated the Delimiting and Priority Indices for each of these PPAs to develop a decision rule that then was compared to the actual decisions that were made and implemented by project personnel. Frequency distributions were used to determine optimal thresholds for each index.

The **Delimiting Index Threshold** was set at 1.2 due to the following: more than 80 percent of PPAs that actually were delimited (versus being treated) had a Delimit Index value of less than 1.2, while more than 80 percent of the PPAs that eventually were treated (versus being delimited) had a Delimit Index greater than 1.2 (Fig. 4.8). The **Priority Index Threshold** was set at 2.8. This threshold likewise had a dual effect in that more than 80 percent of the PPAs for which there was no treatment had a priority index of less than 2.8, while more than 80 percent of the PPAs for which a treatment was implemented had a priority index greater than 2.8 (Fig. 4.9). Both of these indices are used jointly to assign a decision. For example, high moth counts could result in a priority index score that exceeds the threshold of 2.8, which suggests a treatment. However, if the delimiting index is below 1.2, which suggests that the trap-grid density is insufficient to precisely delimit the extent of the infestation; the recommendation would be to delimit. The interaction between the delimiting and priority indices is shown in Figure 4.10.

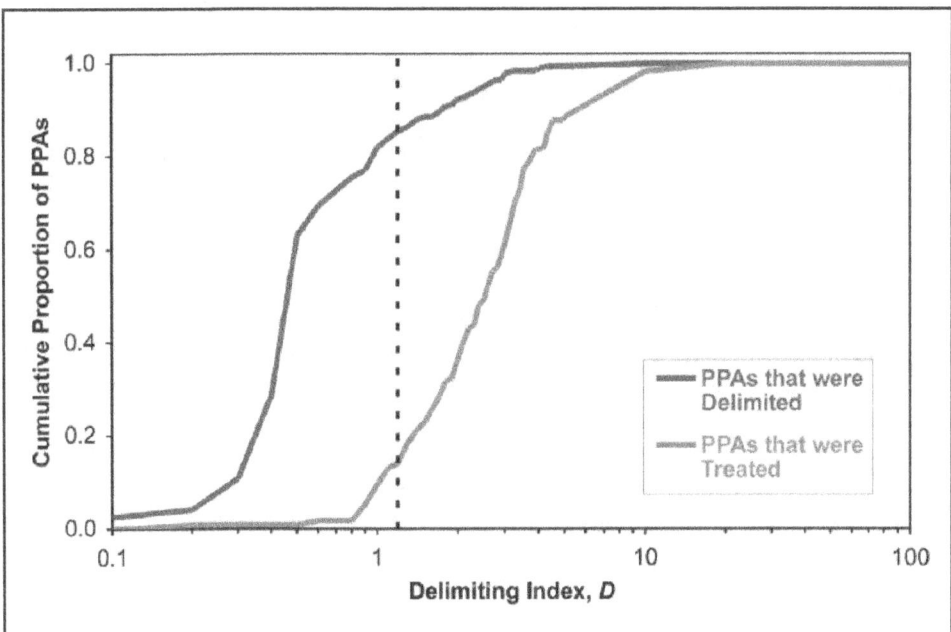

Figure 4.8.—*Cumulative proportion of PPAs that were delimited or treated in Virginia, West Virginia, and North Carolina (1996-2000) based on the Delimiting Index calculated by the Decision Algorithm. The dashed vertical line indicates a Delimiting Index Threshold of 1.2 (from Figure 8A in Tobin et al. 2004).*

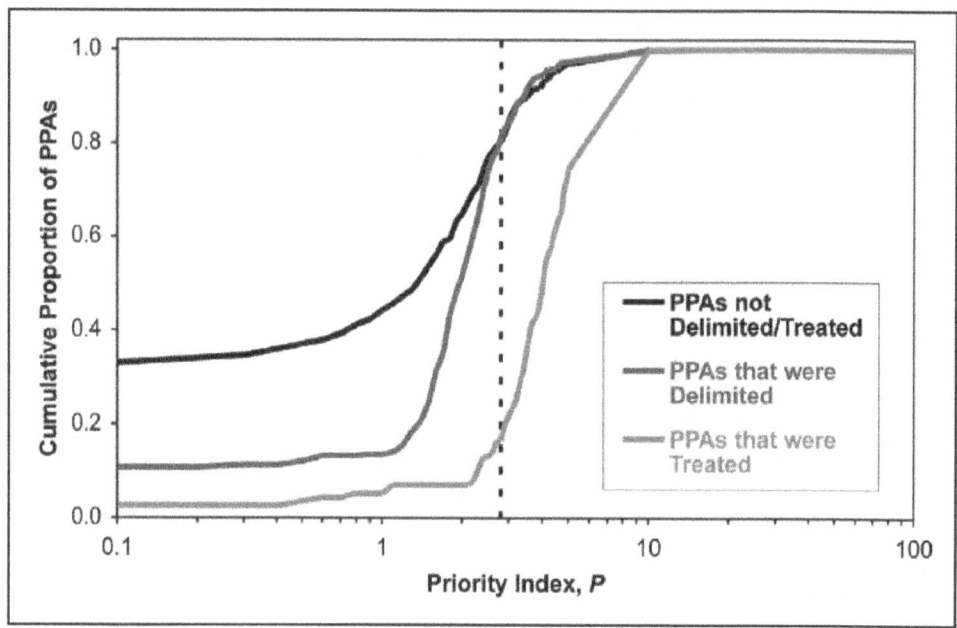

Figure 4.9.—*Cumulative proportion of PPAs that were delimited, treated, or unmanaged in Virginia, West Virginia, and North Carolina (1996-2000) based on the Priority Index calculated by the Decision Algorithm. The dashed vertical line indicates a Priority Index Threshold of 2.8 (from Figure 8B in Tobin et al. 2004).*

Deviating from the Decision Algorithm Recommendations

The Decision Algorithm analyzes data from pheromone-baited traps deployed under STS to make recommendations that best mimic actual decisions by project personnel. However, managers sometimes override these recommendations for various reasons. For example, the Decision Algorithm does not and could not consider the economics of the STS Program, e.g., changes in operating budgets allocated in support of STS. A summary of the deviations that have been observed in the STS Program from 1996 to 2005 is presented in Figure 4.11.

We sometimes tend to deviate from the Decision Algorithm by taking a more aggressive position. In some areas in which moth counts may be low, we may decide to delimit or even treat based on other considerations, such as the detection of life stages through surveys, or if the area has a high risk of gypsy moth population growth and spread, e.g., the presence of nursery stock or a high abundance of preferred host tree types. For example, for areas in which life stages such as egg masses are detected, we usually treat the area in the following year. Life-stage data are not included in the Decision Algorithm because, unlike the situation with traps deployed under STS, they are not collected systematically due to the high costs of these types of surveys. Conversely, we may adopt a less aggressive approach due to budget shortfalls, or in areas that may have a low risk of population growth or spread.

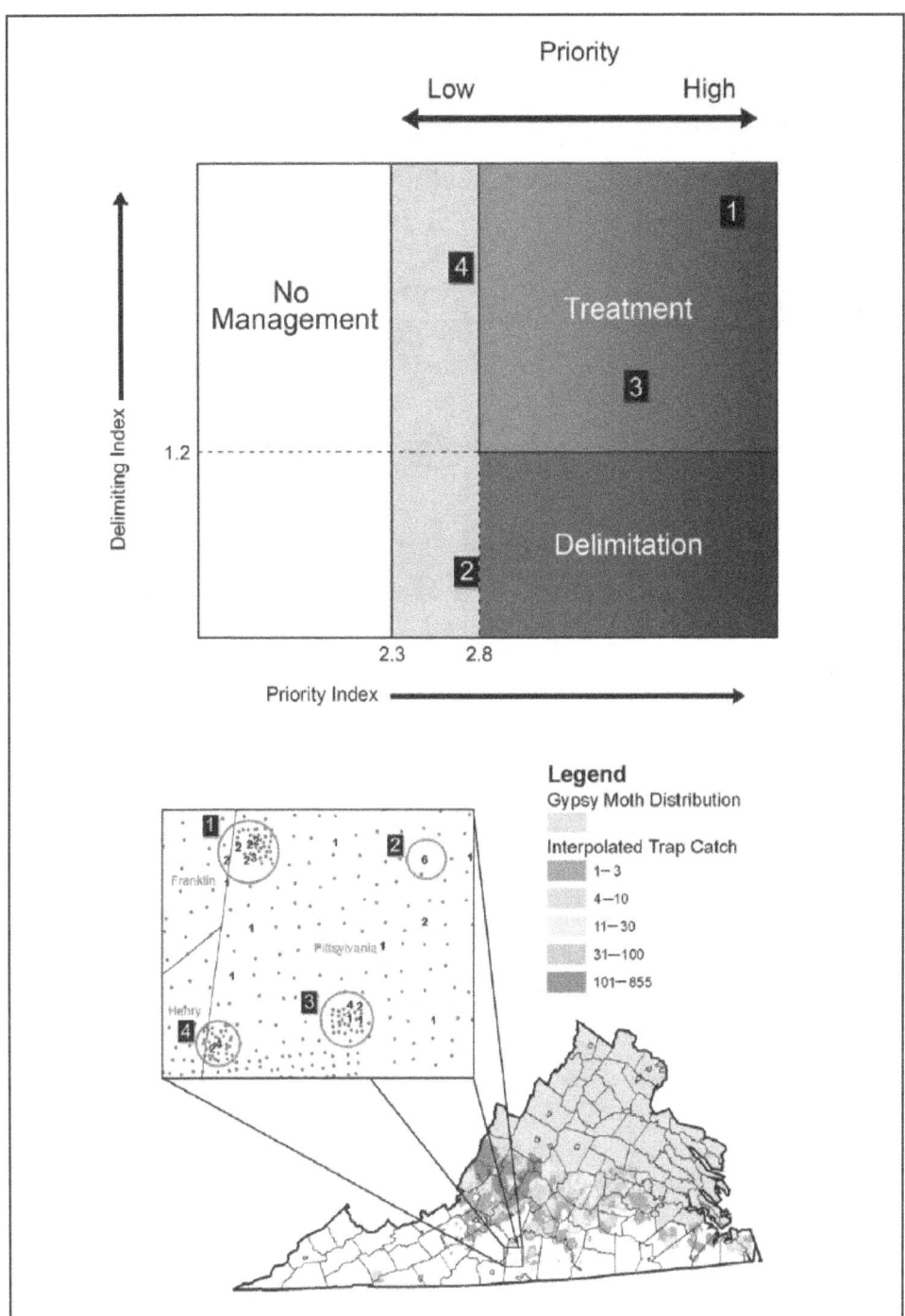

Figure 4.10.—*Relationship between the Delimiting and Priority Indices, using four PPAs identified by the Decision Algorithm in 1999 from Pittsylvania County, Virginia. The Delimiting Index Threshold is 1.2, below which PPAs generally lack a sufficient trap-grid density with which to precisely delimit the spatial extent of the population. The Priority Index Threshold is 2.8, above which PPAs have been treated. However, Priority Index values between 2.3 and 2.8 denote a "gray area" and, depending on available resources, one must decide to treat or delimit PPAs in this area.*

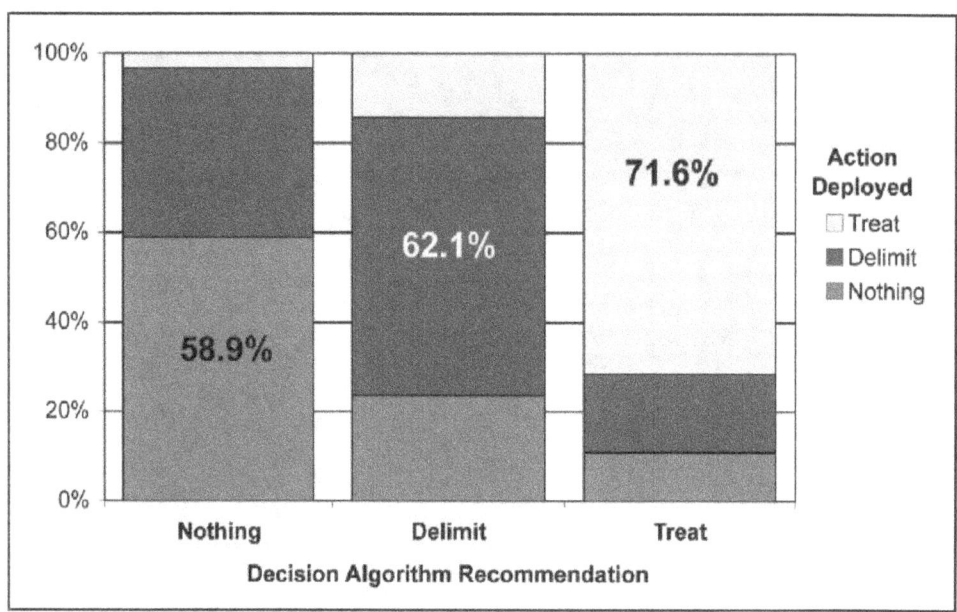

Figure 4.11.—*Decision Algorithm recommendations versus the action deployed under STS (1996-2005; N = 4,329 PPAs). The percentages indicate the frequency with which there is exact agreement between the Decision Algorithm and decisions by STS Program personnel.*

Conclusion

In this chapter we focused on the methods used by the Decision Algorithm to analyze trap-catch data, statistically highlight potential isolated infestations of gypsy moth colonies within the transition zone, and quantify indices that are used in gypsy moth management decisions. The Decision Algorithm also is used to evaluate the efficacy of treatments under the STS Program for eradicating isolated gypsy moth colonies, evaluating the overall effectiveness of the project, and setting boundaries for the project in the next year. These aspects of the Decision Algorithm are discussed in Chapter 5.

Chapter 5. The Decision Algorithm: Project Evaluation

Patrick C. Tobin[1], Alexei A. Sharov[2], and Kevin W. Thorpe[3]

Gypsy Moth Control Tactics Used In Slow the Spread

The Slow the Spread (STS) Program can use only chemical or biological pesticides that were analyzed and were part of the record of decisions under the gypsy moth Final Environmental Impact Statement (EIS) (USDA 1995). The alternatives available are broad strategies developed to meet the needs of a national management program for gypsy moth. Six treatment options are available for use, alone or in combination. They are discussed specifically in Volume II of the Final EIS, as are the effects of treatments on human health and safety, and their potential ecological and environmental effects (USDA 1995). Treatment options include: 1) *Bacillus thuringiensis* variety *kurstaki* (Btk), 2) the gypsy moth nucleopolyhedrosis virus (NPV), registered as Gypchek®, 3) the insect growth regulator diflubenzuron (registered as Dimilin®), 4) mass trapping, 5) mating disruption, and 6) release of sterile insects.

Under STS, two principle tactics are used to manage gypsy moth infestations: Btk and mating disruption using commercial pheromone formulations. Btk has been targeted most often against higher-density infestations; mating disruption is used over larger treatment blocks. For example, from 1996 to 2004, the average treatment block size for Btk and mating disruption blocks was 394 and 1,400 acres, respectively. Average moth density, measured as male moths per trap, was nine for Btk blocks and four for mating disruption blocks (Fig. 5.1). In certain cases, other tactics are used, e.g., Dimilin® or Gypchek®. The acreage treated with each tactic over time is summarized in Table 5.1.

Bacillus thuringiensis is a naturally occurring soil microbe that is used to control a number of insect species across several taxa. Different varieties of this organism produce a protein that is toxic to the target insect when ingested. The *kurstaki* variety is specific to Lepidoptera, such as the gypsy moth. Btk treatments under STS are applied aerially to foliage. Btk often is the tactic of choice when infestations are higher in abundance, i.e., generally maximum pheromone-baited trap catch within the block > 30, or when life stages (egg masses) have been documented. For additional information on the use of Btk under STS, see Reardon et al. (1994).

[1] USDA Forest Service, Northern Research Station, 180 Canfield Street, Morgantown, West Virginia 26505.
[2] Laboratory of Genetics, National Institute on Aging (NIA/NIH), 333 Cassell Drive, Suite 3000, Baltimore, Maryland 21224.
[3] USDA Agricultural Research Service, Insect Biocontrol Laboratory, Building 011A Barc-West, Beltsville, Maryland 20705.

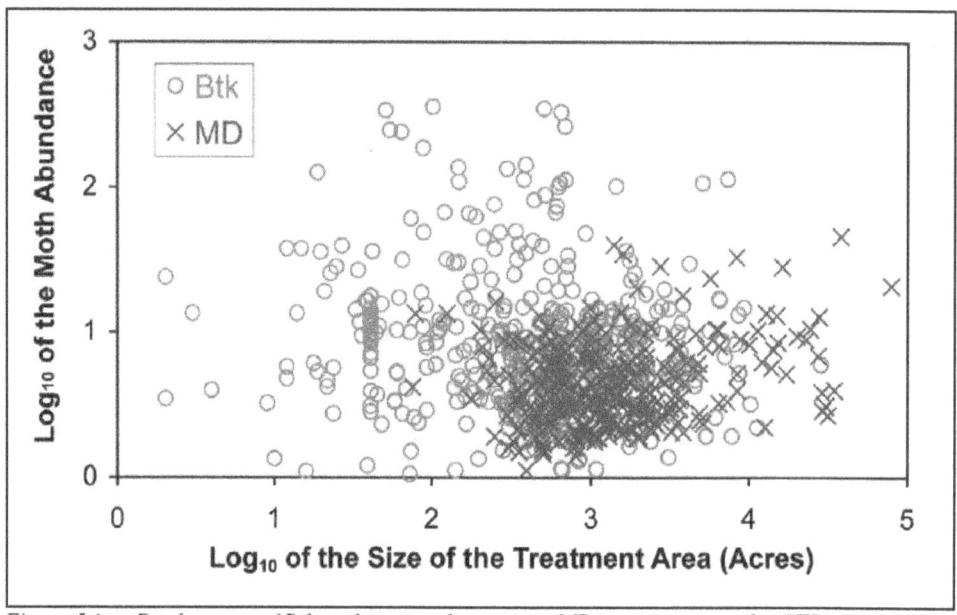

Figure 5.1.—*Deployment of Btk and mating disruption (MD) treatments under STS (1996-2004). Btk is used more often in smaller blocks with higher moth counts; MD is used more often in larger blocks with lower moth counts.*

Table 5.1.—*Acreage treated under STS Pilot Project (1996-1998) and National STS Program (1999-2005) by control strategy. Percentages across each row sum to 100.*

Year	Btk		Mating disruption		Dimilin®		Gypchek®	
	Acres	Percent[a]	Acres	Percent[a]	Acres	Percent[a]	Acres	Percent[a]
1996	24,129	64.2	12,215	32.5	1,216	3.2	0	0.0
1997	66,707	86.1	10,813	13.9	0	0.0	0	0.0
1998	70,112	74.4	24,140	25.6	0	0.0	0	0.0
1999	53,385	53.3	40,860	40.8	1,041	1.0	4,910	4.9
2000	85,010	47.8	92,741	52.2	0	0.0	0	0.0
2001	66,387	23.7	212,768	76.0	736	0.3	0	0.0
2002	35,160	5.9	559,295	93.5	3,924	0.7	0	0.0
2003	75,521	11.7	563,370	87.1	0	0.0	8,004	1.2
2004	123,526	25.8	346,710	72.4	0	0.0	8,737	1.8
2005	108,611	26.2	287,890	69.5	790	0.2	17,075	4.1
Total	708,548	24.4	2,150,802	74.0	7,707	0.3	38,726	1.3

[a]Values represent the percent of acreage treated with each tactic.

Most of the acreage treated under STS nowadays is done using mating disruption (Table 5.1). Plastic flakes impregnated with synthetic pheromone (Disrupt® II, Hercon® Environmental, Emigsville, PA) are applied aerially to foliage, flooding the air with pheromone which interferes with the male moth's ability to locate females who release sex pheromone to attract male mates. The goal of mating disruption is to prevent male moths from locating females and mating. Mating disruption is used most often to manage low-density populations. In some cases, if a high infestation occurs within a larger area requiring treatment under STS, Btk is used in concert with mating disruption to target the "hot spot" within the mating disruption block. For additional information on the use of mating disruption see Reardon et al. (1998).

Dimilin® is the least used tactic under STS (Table 5.1). As an insect growth regulator, it disrupts the ability to synthesize chitin, an important component of the insect cuticle. When caterpillars grow and molt, Dimilin® prevents new cuticle from developing, resulting in mortality. It is not specific to gypsy moth and can adversely affect other species that molt, including nontarget insects and other arthropods such as crabs and shrimp. However, because of its high efficacy, Dimilin® has been used occasionally under STS to manage high gypsy moth populations, particularly in nonaquatic habitats (see USDA 1995).

NPV, formulated as Gypchek®, can be produced only in vivo and thus is manufactured in only limited quantities by the Department of Agriculture. It is a naturally occurring virus of the gypsy moth and is specific to gypsy moth; hence, it is used in environmentally sensitive habitats. Although used sparingly under STS (Table 5.1), NPV can be used as a control tactic against high-density infestations when there is concern for the nontarget effects of Btk on native Lepidoptera, for example, when gypsy moth infestations overlap with populations of the native and endangered Karner blue butterfly, *Lycaeides melissa samuelis* (see Reardon et al. 1996).

Evaluation of Control Tactics

Control tactics used against gypsy moth in STS are evaluated critically to measure the overall effectiveness of the program and to assist in identifying opportunities for improving management tactics. The Decision Algorithm calculates two indices to measure the efficacy of treatments. The first, the **Index of Treatment Success (T)** (Sharov et al. 2002a), measures the change in the density of the treated population before and after treatment while adjusting for changes in nearby, untreated areas that serve as a "control." The second, the **Index of Colony Presence (C)**, measures the ratio of abundance in the treated population relative to the background population.

Index of Treatment Success

The Index of Treatment Success (T) (Sharov et al. 2002a) is based on the philosophy of Abbott's formula (Abbott 1925). It considers the change in population abundance in the treated area before and after treatment as well as the change in abundance in nearby, untreated areas that serve as a control. For example, if treated populations declined at nearly the same rate as those in the untreated areas, the treatment may not be considered "successful" even though the goal of STS is attained from a management perspective. Because untreated populations likewise declined, it may not be possible to *statistically* attribute the decline in treated populations specifically to the control tactic.

To calculate the Index of Treatment Success, the treated area and surrounding areas are divided into three sections as shown in Figure 5.2a. One section is the actual area that represents the treatment block, which is defined by the Decision Algorithm and/or project personnel. The next section is a buffer zone, which is the surrounding area within 1.5 km of the treatment block or other nearby treatment blocks. The buffer zone is not used in the treatment analysis. The last section is the untreated control area. The size of the untreated control area varies according to the size of the treatment block. If both the length and width of the treatment block are less than 12 km, the untreated control area is a region that forms a 24- by 24-km area around the treatment block. However, if the width or height of the treatment block is larger than 12 km, the control area is simply twice the width and length of the treatment block. Then a 0.5-km grid is set over the treatment block and control area (Fig. 5.2b). Cells that include the treatment block are considered <u>treatment cells</u>. Neighboring cells (up to a distance of 1.5 km) are <u>buffer cells</u> and the other cells are <u>control cells</u>. Moth counts from pheromone-baited traps are interpolated in the 0.5-km grid of cells using a spatial interpolation technique called median indicator kriging (Deutsch and Journel 1992).

The Index of Treatment Success, T, is calculated according to

$$T = 1 - \left(\frac{N_{post\text{-}treatment}}{N_{pre\text{-}treatment}} \times \frac{C_{pre\text{-}treatment}}{C_{post\text{-}treatment}} \right), \tag{5.1}$$

where N is the average moth count in the treatment block (pre- or post-treatment), and C is the average moth count in the untreated control block (pre- or post-treatment). For all non-mating disruption treatment blocks in which larvae are targeted during the spring, post-treatment evaluation, which is based on male moth catch during the summer, is

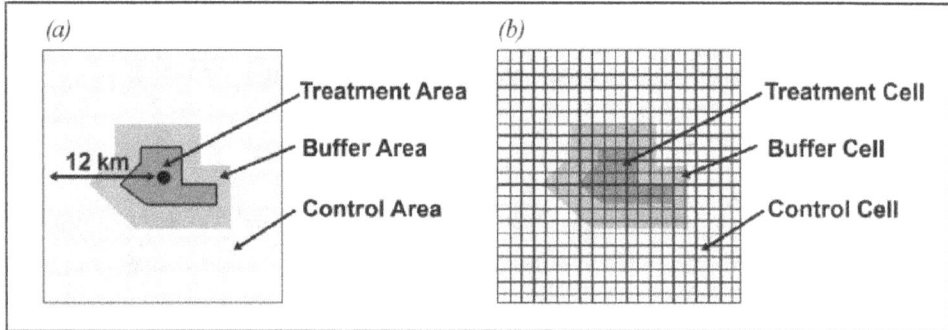

Figure 5.2.—*(a) Control areas around a treatment block are at least 24 by 24 km and centered on the area to be treated. The entire area is then divided into 500-m grid cells (b), which are assigned to the treatment, buffer, or control area. Moth counts are interpolated over the entire area and values from the treatment and control areas are used to calculate the Index of Treatment Success. Values from the buffer cells are not used.*

conducted later in the year. However, in mating disruption blocks, post-treatment evaluations are done in the year after treatment since this control tactic targets the adults; hence, measurements of the efficacy of this tactic cannot be estimated until the following year.

Depending on the value of T, there are three resulting scenarios: 1) values of T $\geq$ 0.67 denote a successful treatment because there was a reduction of at least 67 percent in moth counts in the treated block after adjusting for changes in the untreated control block; hence, the STS goal was obtained; 2) values of T between 0.34 and 0.66 indicate that the treatment was partially successful. Although moth counts in the treated block declined more than those in the untreated control, the rate of reduction was below the STS goal; and 3) values of T $\leq$ 0.33 denote a treatment failure because moth counts in the treated block did not decline significantly more than those in untreated controls.

It is important to note that the classification of a treatment as successful, as measured by T, does not necessarily mean that the colony has been eradicated. For example, if the initial population numbers were high, several successful treatments may be needed to eradicate the colony. Also, if the moth population in the nearby control areas exploded, populations in the treated area may have increased but still provided a T value of 0.67 or greater. An example of the dynamics between control and treated blocks is shown in Figure 5.3. The Index of Treatment Success (T) measures the success of intervention activity against the gypsy moth under STS, but is intended to be used in concert with other evaluation measures to assess the quality of the program, particularly at local spatial scales. For additional information on treatment evaluation under STS, see Sharov et al. (2002a).

The average, project-wide calculations for the Index of Treatment Success is summarized in Figure 5.4; summary by treatment strategy (Btk and mating disruption) is shown in Figure 5.5. Although mating disruption treatment blocks have had higher index scores overall (Fig. 5.5a) as well as generally higher scores over time (Fig. 5.5b), it is not valid to compare treatment strategies based on this index alone since Btk and mating disruption are deployed differently. The former is used more often with higher density infestations (Fig. 5.1). Often, higher density populations require repeated treatments to eliminate the colony, in these blocks, the Index of Treatment Success would suggest a "failure." This index is a valid tool for evaluating the efficacy of our treatment strategies and helping project personnel identify infestations that require repeated management tactics.

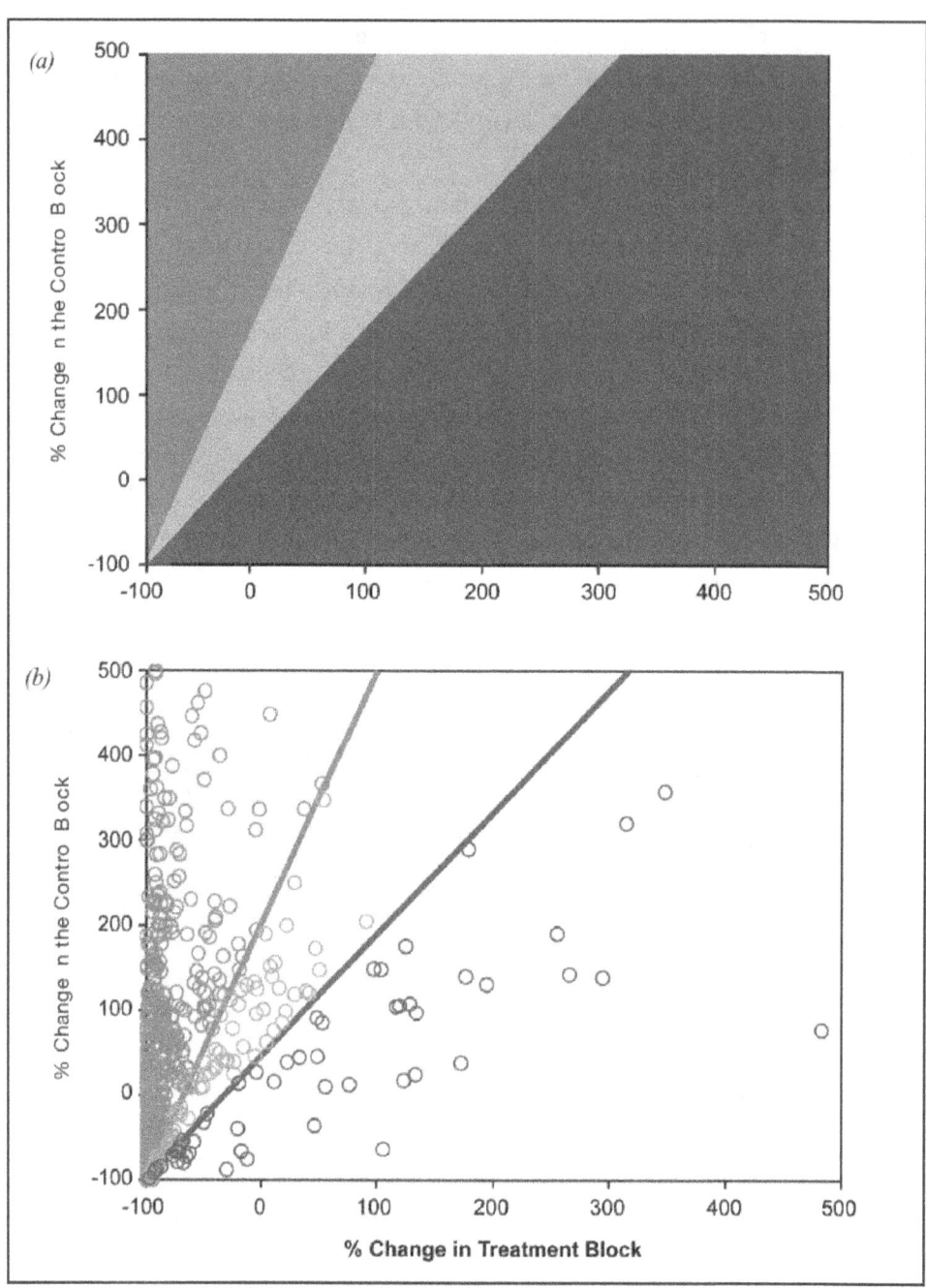

Figure 5.3.—*The relationship between moth abundance in treated and untreated control blocks is critical when evaluating the Index of Treatment Success. In (a), red areas indicate "successful" treatments, blue areas represent "failures," while gray areas are "partial successes." Theoretically, populations in the treated block can increase in abundance but the treatment still can be considered successful if untreated control populations explode. In contrast, treated populations can decline but the treatment can be considered a failure if untreated populations collapse dramatically. (b) shows these same thresholds with actual data from treatment/control blocks managed under STS from 1996 to 2004.*

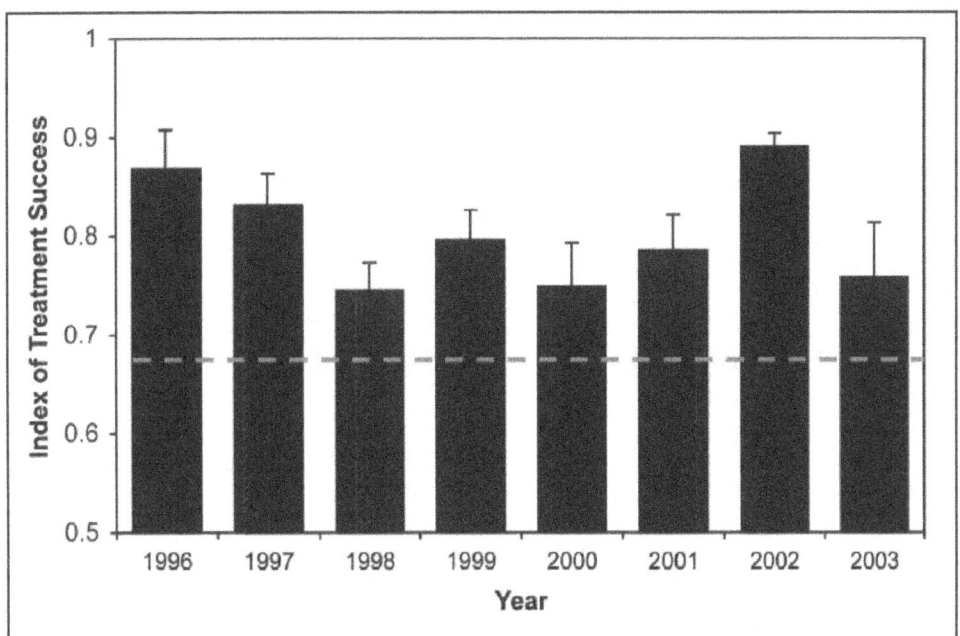

Figure 5.4.—*Average (+SE) value of the Index of Treatment Success for the STS Program, 1996 to 2003. The dashed red line indicates the STS Program Goal of 0.67, which corresponds to a 67-percent reduction in moth counts in the treated area after adjusting for changes in nearby, untreated control areas.*

Index of Colony Presence

Another goal of managing isolated colonies under STS is to reduce population numbers to the background level in the neighboring areas. In the areas far beyond the population front, the background moth counts in pheromone-baited traps are nearly zero. Thus, the colonies that are found in these areas should be eradicated, i.e., moth captures reduced to zero. However, in areas more proximal to the population front, the background moth counts may be one to two moths per trap. Therefore, another goal of colony management is not necessarily a complete eradication but at least a reduction of moth counts to the background level. The **Index of Colony Presence (C)** is used to evaluate treatments with respect to the goal of reducing moth counts in the treatment block to those of the background level. It is calculated as the ratio of the average moth captures in the treatment block (N_{t+1}) and the control block (C_{t+1}) in the year (or second year in the case of mating disruption) following the treatment:

$$C = \left(\frac{N_{t+1}}{C_{t+1}} \right). \tag{5.2}$$

When $C = 1$, moth counts in the treatment block are the same as those in the control area, and the goal of colony management is met. When $C > 1$, additional

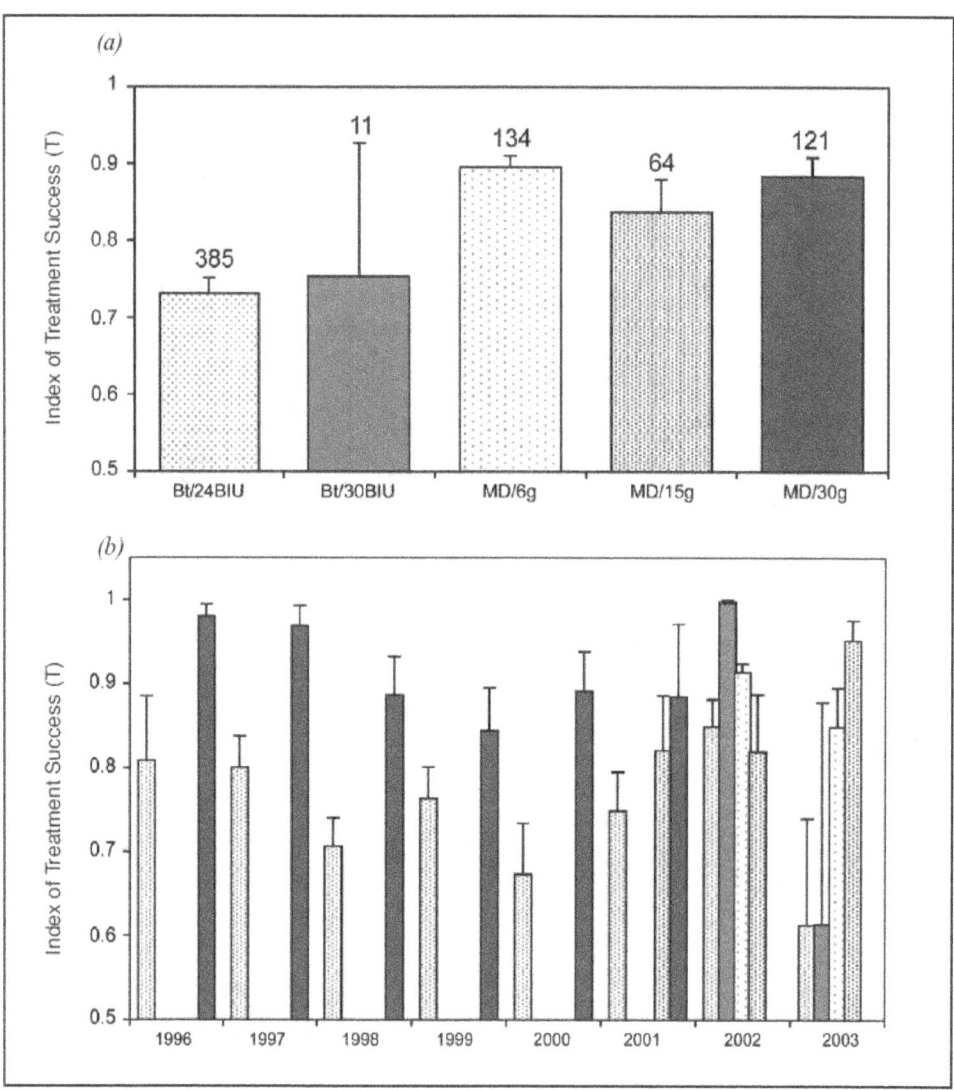

Figure 5.5.—*Averages (+SE) of the Index of Treatment Success for the STS Program by (a) treatment strategy and dose (Bt = Btk, BIU = billion International Units, MD = mating disruption; BIU and g indicate the dose per acre), which is also displayed—using the same color scheme—in (b) from 1996 to 2003. In (a), the numbers above the error bars represent the sample size (number of treatment blocks). Because these two management tactics are used differently (cf. Figure 5.1), the two cannot be compared.*

treatments may be necessary in the following year. It is possible to obtain a value of C > 1 in a block that was treated successfully according to the index of Treatment Success (T). This means that, although the treatment was successful, additional ones are needed. For example, colonies with a high moth abundance may require successive treatments to bring the value of C to 1. Each successful treatment generally reduces the value of C. However, projectwide, there is a relationship between the Index of Treatment Success and the Index of Colony Presence (Fig. 5.6). Therefore, the latter is considered as an indicator of long-term success in managing a colony.

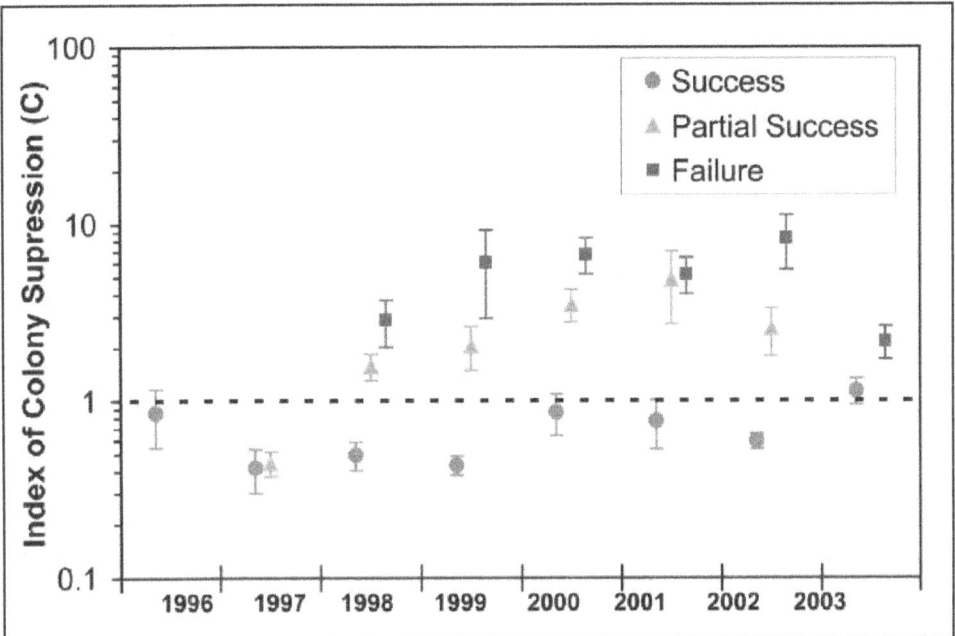

Figure 5.6.—*The Index of Colony Presence generally is less than 1 when treated populations are reduced to the level of nearby, background populations. Note how the values of this Index, from 1996 to 2003, relate to the Index of Treatment Success (categorized into treatment success, partial success, or failure).*

Evaluating Gypsy Moth Spread

Evaluating gypsy moth spread is the second principle evaluation component calculated by the Decision Algorithm and used in evaluating the STS Program. For this component, the Decision Algorithm estimates the boundaries of moth abundance thresholds, calculates the distance between these thresholds in successive years, and averages the distances to determine rates of spread. These rates can be expressed as both projectwide and region specific.

Estimating Moth Population Boundaries

Delineating population boundaries is important for estimating rates of population spread and managing population spread, e.g., planning quarantine zones. The first step in estimating the rate of spread is to delimit the boundaries of the estimated 1-, 3-, 10-, 30-, 100-, and 300-moth abundance thresholds. These are thresholds at which gypsy moth abundance generally occurs. For example, the 10-moth abundance threshold, or 10-moth line, delineates where moth counts to the east and the north of boundary generally exceed 10 moths/trap, while counts to the south and west, the directions in which gypsy moth is spreading, generally are fewer than 10 moths/trap.

In actuality, population boundaries derived from interpolations based on trap-catch data are irregular, with "islands," "lakes," and "folds" common on each side of the moth line. Irregular boundaries can be difficult to analyze. Instead, trap-catch data are used to optimize the location of the various moth abundance thresholds by the **Best Cell Classification Method** (Fig. 5.7). This method is based on work by Sharov et al. (1995b) in which different approaches to estimating boundaries from STS trap-catch data were compared. The **Best Cell Classification Method** was considered the optimal technique.

Aside from their use in estimating gypsy moth spread, moth population boundaries also are used to set project boundaries. As mentioned previously, gypsy moth can be separated spatially into an **infested zone** that is continuously occupied, the **transition zone** where isolated colonies become established, and an **uninfested zone** (see Fig. 2.6). The transition zone, which is managed by the STS Program, can be further divided into **Action** and **Monitoring Areas** (see Fig. 3.1). The moth abundance thresholds, particularly the 10-moth line, which generally is the least variable among all the population boundaries (Sharov et al. 1997b), are used directly to set these boundaries (Fig. 5.8).

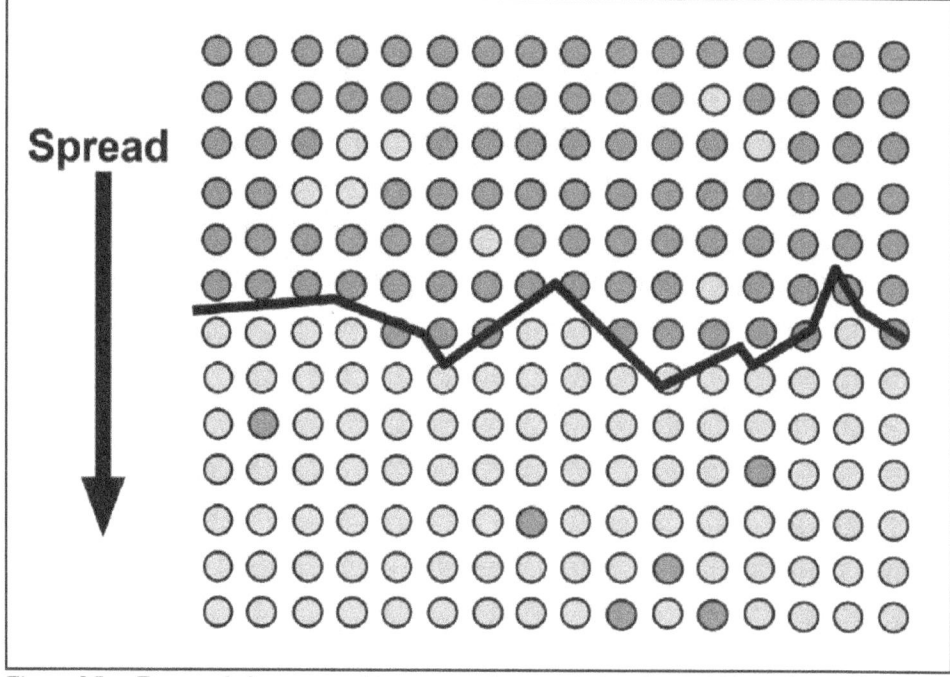

Figure 5.7.—*Trap-catch data are used in constructing population threshold boundaries. For example, assume that the red dots indicate traps in which the catch was 10 or more moths, while gray dots indicate those in which fewer than 10 moths were caught, and we want to delineate the 10-moth abundance threshold (10-moth line). Since population boundaries are irregular, there almost always will be misclassified locations (gray dots mixed with red dots and vice versa). The Best Cell Classification Method optimizes the boundary location to minimize misclassified locations on either side of the boundary. This is repeated for each abundance threshold: 1-, 3-, 10-, 30-, 100-, and 300-moth lines.*

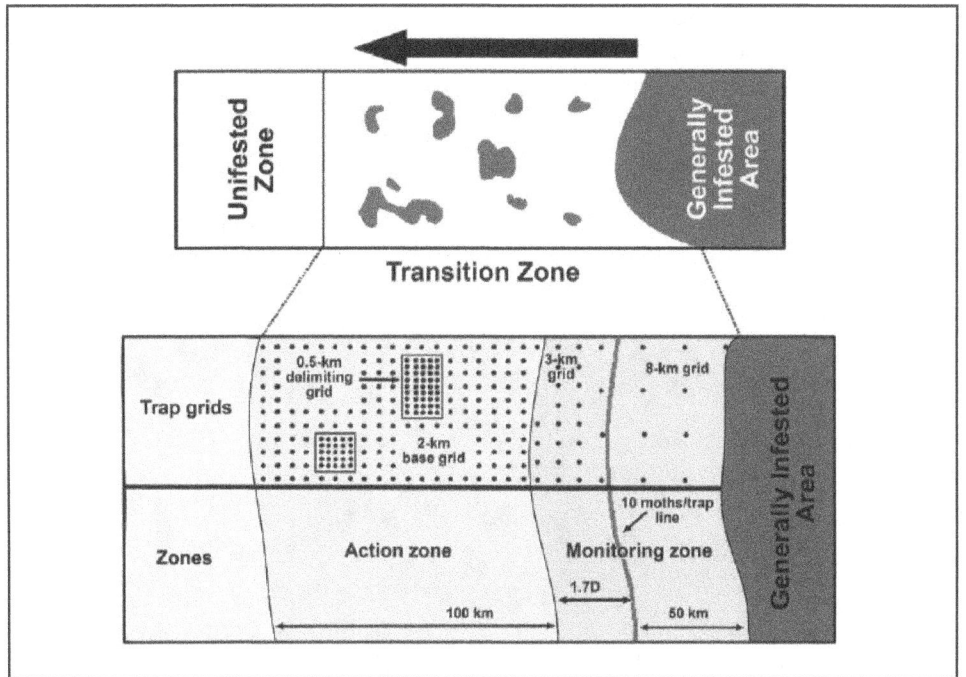

Figure 5.8.—*Moth abundance thresholds are also used to define boundaries of the STS Program area. The 10-moth line is the least variable boundary in space and time, and is approximately 50 km from the generally infested area. The beginning of the Action Zone (the Action Zone boundary most proximal to the generally infested area) is set at 1.7 D km from the 10-moth line, where D is dynamic and is the distance between the 10- and 30-moth lines. If the 30-moth line is unavailable, the 3-moth line is used. The Action Zone itself is approximately 100 km wide (from Figure 1 in Tobin et al. 2004).*

Estimating Gypsy Moth Spread

Once moth abundance thresholds are delineated, the distance between each threshold in consecutive years, e.g., the distance between the 10-moth line in year t and $t+1$, is calculated from a fixed point in space at transects radiating from the fixed point at intervals of 1° (Sharov et al. 1995b, Tobin et al. 2007). Then the distances for each of the six thresholds (1-, 3-, 10-, 30-, 100-, and 300-moth abundance thresholds) are averaged to determine the **Rate of Spread** (see Fig. 5.9). The rate of spread is then compared to the historical, pre-STS average of 20 km/yr to determine the degree of reduction. STS has a target spread rate of 10 km/yr, or a 50 percent reduction, from the historical average (cf. Liebhold et al. 1992).

In addition to rates of spread, we also are interested in the **Interboundary Distance**, which is the distance among population threshold boundaries (Fig. 5.10). Simple models suggest that interboundary distances should be proportional to the rate of population spread. Long-distance dispersal of the gypsy moth is due primarily to inadvertent transportation of life stages. After an isolated colony is established, its growth is

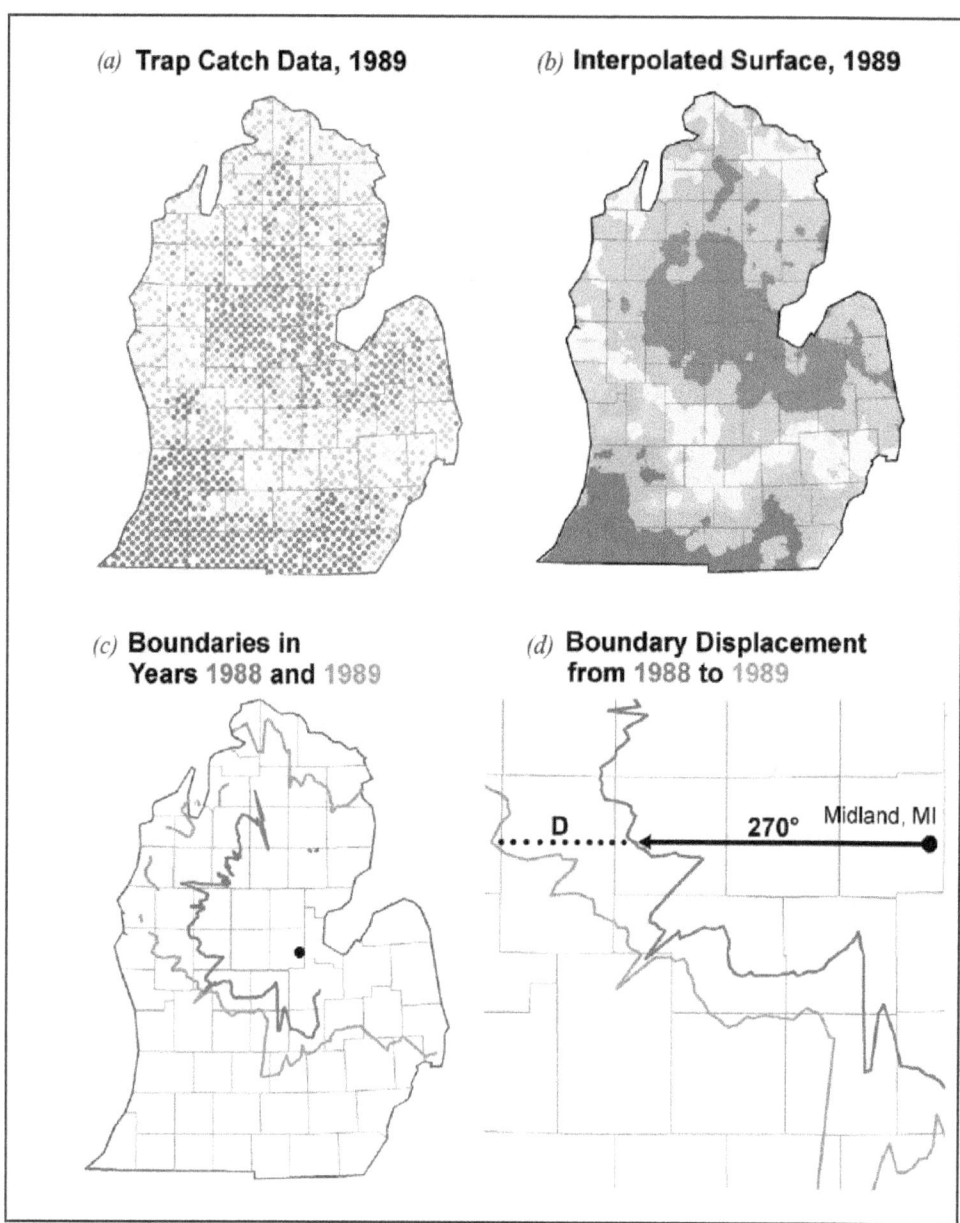

Figure 5.9.—*To measure the yearly rate of gypsy moth spread, trap-catch data from pheromone-baited traps (a) are used in geostatistical methods to interpolate abundance (b). An optimization method (Sharov et al. 1995) is then used to estimate population threshold boundaries based on the interpolated surface (c). The displacement, D, between threshold boundaries from year* t-1 *to year* t *is measured using radiating transects, at 1° intervals, from a fixed point (d). In the example above, the fixed point is Midland, the approximate location of the initial gypsy moth introduction in Michigan, and one of the transects is shown (270°). Displacements from each transect are averaged to estimate the year-to-year rate of spread, and spread rates are calculated for the entire STS Program area as well as for smaller regions (state or sub-state level) within STS (from Figure 5 in Tobin et al. 2007a).*

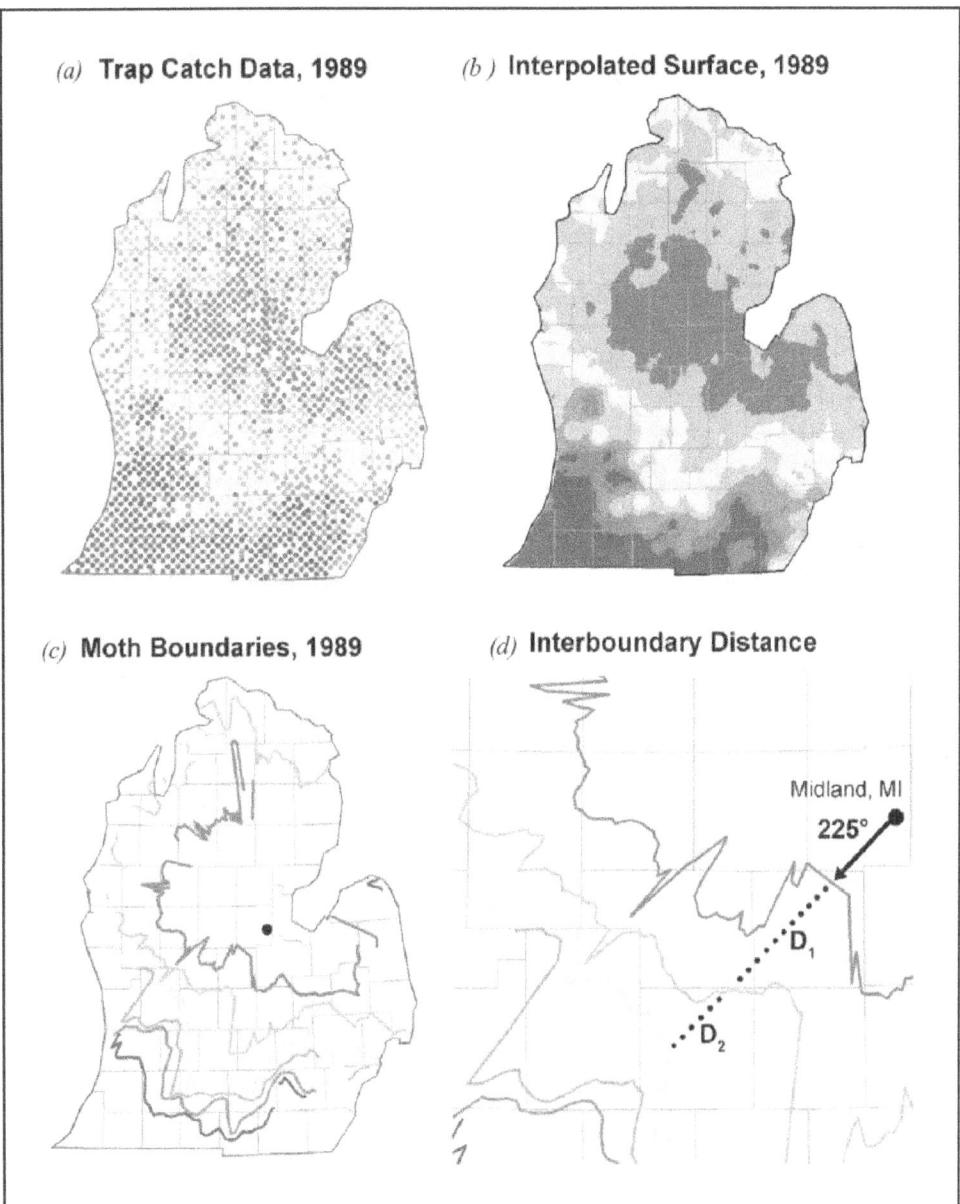

(a) Trap Catch Data, 1989

(b) Interpolated Surface, 1989

(c) Moth Boundaries, 1989

(d) Interboundary Distance

Midland, MI

225°

D_1

D_2

Figure 5.10.—*Trap-catch data from pheromone baited traps (a), from which abundance is interpolated (b) is also used to measure the Interboundary Distance. An optimization method (Sharov et al. 1995) is used to estimate population threshold boundaries (c) of the location at which the interpolated moth catch per trap is 1 (dark blue), 3 (light blue), 10 (green), 30 (yellow), 100 (orange), or 300 (red). The displacement between threshold boundaries is measured using radiating transects, at intervals of 1° from a fixed point (d). In (d), D_1 represents the displacement between the 300- and 100-moth abundance threshold boundary, and D_2 is the displacement between the 100- and 30-moth boundary; both are measured at the 225° transect. Displacements from each transect are averaged to estimate the year-to-year rate of Interboundary Distance. Simple models show that Interboundary Distances are proportional to the rate of spread. Thus, "boundary compression" generally occurs if spread is being reduced.*

autonomous and does not depend on subsequent immigration. Thus, we assume that the rate of population growth in this colony does not depend on the age of the colony until the population reaches its carrying capacity and defoliation begins. Given these factors, the interboundary distance should decrease if the rate of spread is being reduced by the STS Program. This effect called "boundary compression," is a critical tool in evaluating the STS Program. Program-wide spread rates by year, 3-year moving averages of spread, and the program-wide trend in interboundary distances are shown in Figure 5.11.

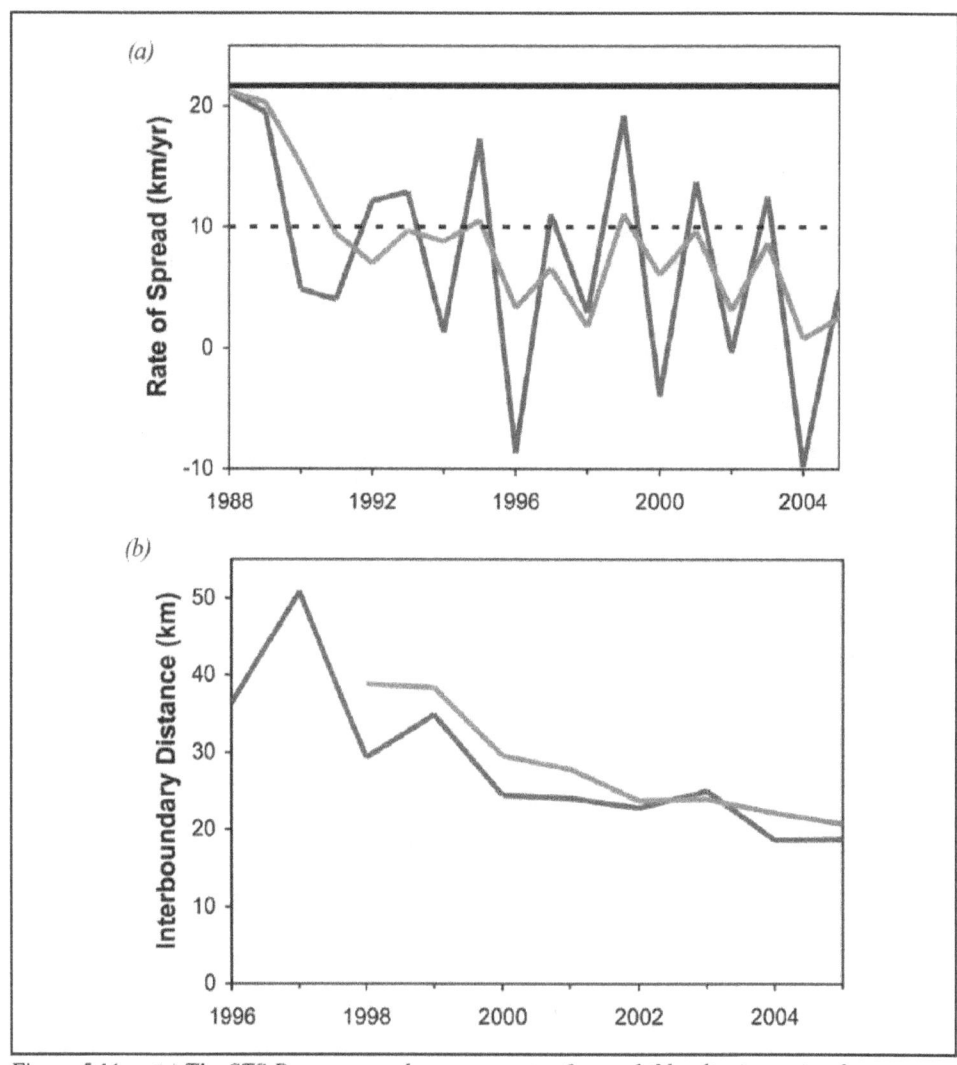

Figure 5.11.—(a) The STS Program yearly average rate of spread (blue line), moving 3-year average spread (red line), historical, pre-STS average spread rate (20.8 km/yr, thick black horizontal line, Liebhold et al. 1992), and STS target spread rate of 10 km/yr (dashed black line) from 1988 to 2005. (b) The STS Program yearly averages of the Interboundary Distance (blue line) and 3-year moving average (red line) from 1996 to 2005. Data prior to 2000 represent pre-STS projects.

Conclusion

In this chapter we focused on the methods used by the Decision Algorithm to evaluate the efficacy of treatments that are deployed under the STS Program to eradicate isolated gypsy moth colonies, evaluate the overall effectiveness of the project, and set boundaries for the project in the next year. The Decision Algorithm, a critical component of the STS Program, relies on extensive areawide survey data and computationally intensive data processing to objectively quantify spatial and temporal population patterns to achieve areawide management of expanding gypsy moth populations. It also is a living algorithm that is updated continuously to improve the manner in which it processes data, makes recommendations, and evaluates the project.

Chapter 6 addresses the database management structure and information delivery of the STS Program. The Decision Algorithm automatically generates a series of web pages that can be used interactively to visualize maps of trap locations and interpolated surfaces, phenological predictions of gypsy moth life stages, and treatment recommendations and evaluation. This information allows state participants to view their own data easily, and can be used to educate the general public about the program in their area.

Chapter 6. Data Management and Information Delivery

Amos H. Ziegler[1] and E. Anderson Roberts[2]

Introduction

Data management and information delivery are an integrative framework for the Slow the Spread (STS) Program. The operational procedures discussed in Chapters 3 through 5 focused on monitoring, determining potential problem areas, and project evaluation. The data management and information delivery infrastructure uses cutting-edge technologies to manage and deliver derived products to cooperators and project management. Raw trapping data is validated and loaded into the project's distributed database where it drives the decision-support system. Trapping and decision-support system products are disseminated to users through the project's Internet data portals. This integrative technological framework has been developed and is managed by the Slow the Spread Information Systems Group.

Composed of personnel from Virginia Tech and Michigan State University, the STS Information Systems Group develops and supports the database management, GIS, and information distribution activities of the STS Program (Fig. 6.1). Data management and information delivery are the backbone of the STS data flow and have played a key role in the project's successful transition from a pilot project to a national management strategy.

In this chapter we review and discuss the management of trap data by cooperators from the point of submission to the distributed project database. This includes the validation of submitted trap data, the correction of subsequent data errors, data integration with the STS GIS, and the delivery of data products through the project's Internet information portals to cooperators, project personnel, and the general public. We also discuss the structure and function of the trapping and spatial databases as well as the information technology (IT) that is used to achieve analysis and visualization, data and product delivery, cooperator-project integration, and the maximization of data ownership for cooperators.

[1] Michigan State University, Department of Entomology, Computational Ecology and Visualization Laboratory, 1405 South Harrison Road, 209 Manly Miles Building, East Lansing, Michigan 48824
[2] Virginia Polytechnic Institute and State University, 315 Price Hall, Department of Entomology, Blacksburg, Virginia 24061

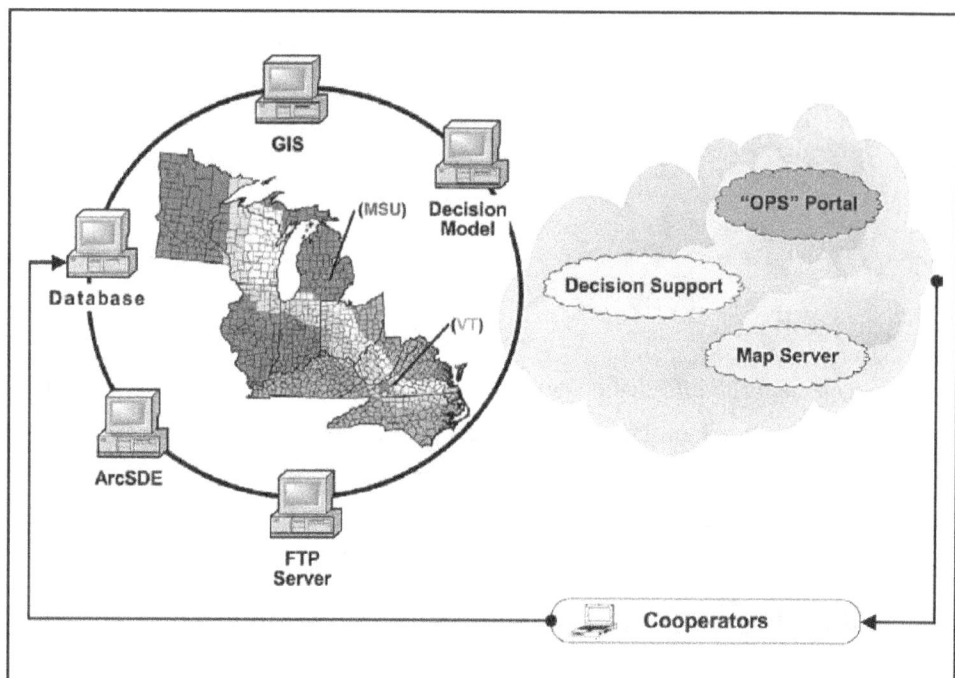

Figure 6.1.—*Cooperators interact with the STS Information Systems Groups at Michigan State University (MSU) and Virginia Tech (VT) through Internet-based resources.*

Data Management

The STS Program uses the Oracle Enterprise Edition relational database management system (RDBMS). This software, which has been used projectwide since 1996, provides the advanced management and replication environment necessary to manage the distributed STS database. The Oracle software is used to manage the tabular trapping database and supports the management of spatial data through the integration with software from ESRI and Arc Spatial Database Engine (ArcSDE). Currently, the integration of Oracle with ArcSDE to manage the spatial component of the project is a separate application from the Oracle RDBMS housing the trapping database.

The trapping databases at Information Systems Groups at Virginia Tech and Michigan State University are cross-replicated on a nightly basis to provide fault tolerance and data backup. Additional offline backups are completed every 12 hours and a backup is taken offsite each evening. The databases at both locations use a staggered deployment strategy for implementing major revisions of the Oracle Enterprise Edition software. This staggering provides an additional level of fault tolerance for the distributed STS database in the event of a fatal software bug or unforeseen incompatibility with the production IT infrastructure.

The STS data management philosophy is one of central management with an accompanying high degree of cooperator access. The STS Program has succeeded largely because of a policy that grants cooperators a high level of data access that, in turn, fosters a greater sense of data ownership. We have found that this data management philosophy develops the greatest level of participation by current cooperators and provides a smoother transition into the project for new cooperators.

Structure

The STS trapping and spatial databases are composed of standard database objects such as tables, views, constraints, indexes, triggers, procedures, functions, and foreign and primary keys (Table 6.1). Some of these objects are found in many simple desktop database systems (tables, indexes, keys), but more sophisticated database objects are within enterprise class systems such as that used by the STS database (Oracle Enterprise Edition). The functions of the objects used in the STS databases are varied and each plays a role in the data life cycle (Table 6.2).

Annually, the STS trapping database is preloaded with 70,000 to 90,000 predetermined trapping data records within the STS Program area (Table 3.1). In addition, many traps deployed under state surveys conducted in non-STS areas are included in the trapping data; thus, the total number of traps each year generally exceeds 130,000. During the course of an operational season, these traps are placed in the field within specified tolerances at predetermined trap locations and inspected at least once during the trapping season (Fig. 3.3). Quality control inspections are preformed on at least 10 percent of the placed traps (Fig. 3.4). The raw field data are then submitted to the distributed project database and the management phase of the trapping-data life cycle begins.

Table 6.1.—*Count of distinct database objects*

Database object	Object count
Table	32
View	90
Constraint	360
Index	60
Trigger	20
Procedures and functions	70

Table 6.2.—*Descriptions of database objects*

Object Class	Function
Table	A relational object consisting of one or more fields, where each field is the intersection of a column and a row (record) and has a value based on this specific, logical position. Tables are the primary data holding objects within the database.
View	A logical table, storing no data itself, which allows access to one or more tables on which the view is based. Views are used to create virtual tables in support of the online reporting system developed for viewing raw trapping data.
Constraint	Restrictions on a table column or columns that define allowable values, thus preventing unwanted values from being stored. Constraints are a key element of the data integrity scheme imposed on the database.
Index	A structure that maintains an ordered set of entries, providing fast access to specific values.
Trigger	A PL/SQL program associated with a table's insert, select, or update activity. A trigger executes when the user performs the activity with which it's associated. Triggers are primarily used to "trigger" the validation routines of the temporary data tables.
Procedure	A PL/SQL program with an assigned name that is stored in the database in compiled form. Procedures are the mechanism by which data validations are executed against modified and incoming trapping data.
Function	A piece of code that returns a value and may accept arguments.
Primary Key	A column or set of columns that comprises a primary key constraint.
Foreign Key	A constraint that validates a record by ensuring that the value(s) in the constraining column(s) matches values already existing in some other column(s), either in the same or in a different table. Foreign keys are another element of the data integrity scheme imposed on the database.

Trapping-Data Life Cycle

In the discussion of the STS trapping data life cycle that began in Chapter 3, the authors described the collection of field-trap data using handheld GPS devices, the transfer of field data from field personnel to supervisors, and the uploading of field data from state cooperators to the database nodes for loading into the project's database (Fig. 3.7). Our discussion of the data life cycle continues with descriptions of the field data Autoloader Service, Oracle SQL-Loader, temporary database tables, database validations, cooperator error correction, and permanent database tables (Fig. 6.2). This portion of the data life cycle includes the management phase, while the discussion in Chapter 3 elaborated on the data collection phase of the life cycle. Finally, the tabular trapping data are used to construct spatial data layers that are stored in an ArcSDE-enabled database in support of GIS analysis and visualization.

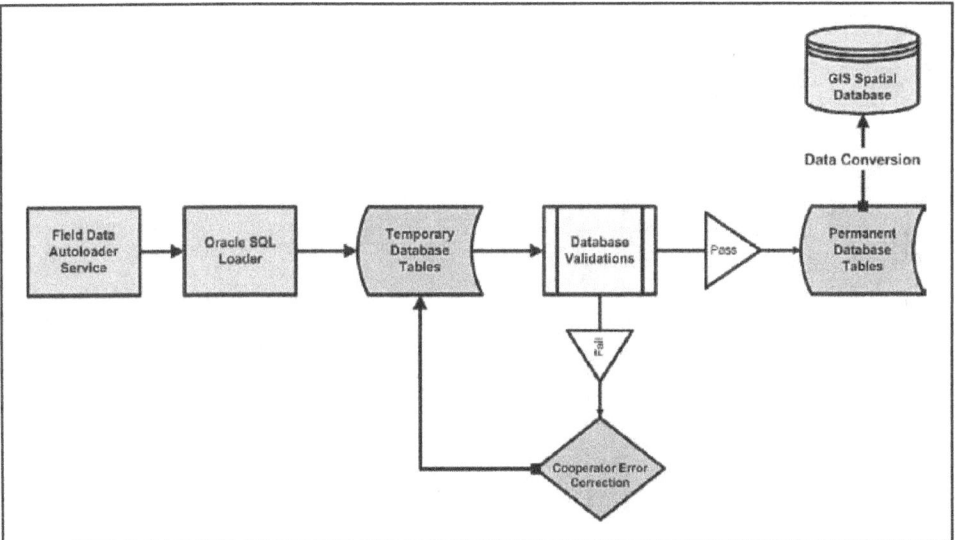

Figure 6.2.—*STS field data life cycle within the trapping database.*

Field Data Autoloader Service

The Autoloader Service is a set of Perl scripts designed to both validate and load raw GPS trapping data into the project database. The service is run automatically every 10 minutes during the trapping season. The scheduled routine handles the database loading, file management, and cooperator notification. Every autoloader job is recorded in dedicated tables in the Oracle database. These tables are used to retain information on the cooperator, date and time, and associated loading errors.

Oracle SQL Loader

The Oracle Bulk Loader is invoked following data validation by the Autoloader service scripts. It uses a control file that defines the structure of the raw GPS file and breaks down the fixed width data using column definitions corresponding to the structure of the temporary database tables (Fig. 6.3).

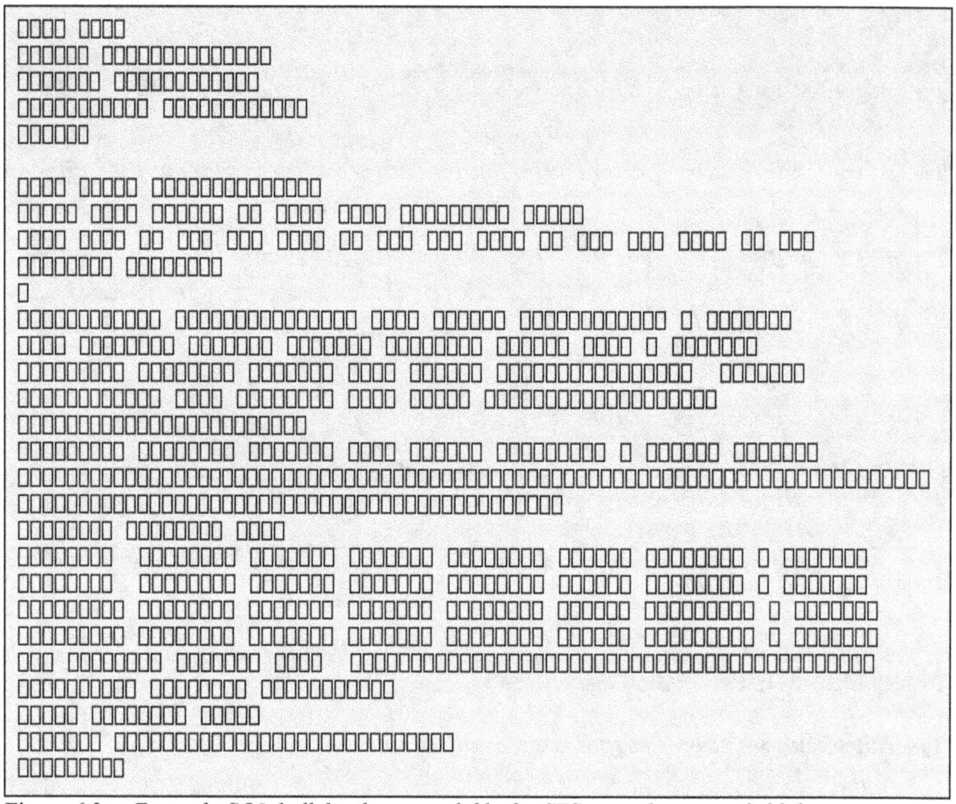

Figure 6.3.—*Example SQL bulk loader control file for STS trap placement field data.*

Temporary Database Tables

The temporary tables are used to hold the raw trapping data for data validation and error correction. These tables reside outside the permanent structure of the project database.

Database Validations

The validations are a rule set that is triggered each time a data record is inserted or updated in the temporary tables. Validations are performed on placement and inspection data for both quad-based and county-based states (Tables 6.3 and 6.4). These thorough validations generate trap data that is highly accurate positionally. Extensively validating the trap data is possible because the trap locations are predetermined rather than responsive in nature. See the *Project Documents* section of the Operations Portal Web site (http://www.gmsts.org/operations/) for details on the validations and codes used in Tables 6.3 and 6.4.

Table 6.3.—*Trap placement validations*

- A record exists with predetermined information for each site.
- Quad code is present and valid.
- County code is present and valid.
- Site number is present and greater than zero.
- Trap placement date is present and valid.
- Trapper initials are present and valid within the agency responsible for the site.
- Trap type is one of the following: D, M, O (delta, milk carton, omit).
- A valid reason is included for each omitted site: H, L, O, W, R, V, S, X, B.
- Each record has a unique quad code and site number.
- UTM coordinates are unique within the UTM zone; each record corresponds to a unique predetermined grid node.

Table 6.4.—*Trap inspection validations*

- Quad code is present and valid.
- County code is present and valid.
- Site number is present and greater than zero.
- A trap placement record exists for this quad and site.
- Inspections should be performed on placed traps.
- Trapper initials are present and valid within the agency responsible for site.
- Each record has a unique quad, site, date, and inspection type.
- All midseason inspection dates are earlier than final inspections.
- Trap condition is one of the following: D, G, I, M (damaged, good, inaccessible, missing).
- If trap condition is D or G, trap catch must be greater than or equal to zero.
- If trap condition is I or M, trap catch should be blank.
- Field check entry, if present, is either a P or F to indicate a quality control inspection.
- If field check entry is F, a valid quality control failure code must be entered (A, C, D, G, I, R, T, U, X, M, S, W).
- Trap check is an M or F (midseason or final).
- Only one final routine inspection may be reported for a site.

Permanent Database Tables

Data records are transferred to the permanent tables if the record passes all of the validations. Conversely, if a data record fails one of the validations, it is retained in the temporary database tables and an error is logged in the error tables.

Cooperator Error Correction

The errors and associated data records in the temporary tables are available to cooperators for error correction through the Operations Portal Web site. Once a data record in error has been corrected, the validations are retriggered and the validation loop is repeated (Fig. 6.2), though errors might remain that need to be corrected.

GIS Spatial Database

Data from the permanent tables of the trapping database are available to the GIS spatial database for conversion into spatial data layers. The spatial database is managed by the ESRI ArcSDE, which allows for the management of feature geometry and attributes associated with the data layers stored in the database. The Oracle RDBMS software used to manage the trapping database is used similarly in managing the spatial database in support of the GIS analysis and visualization.

Spatial-Data Life Cycle

As mentioned previously, data from the permanent tables of the trapping database are the source of raw data for creating layers of trapping data within the GIS database and are used for analysis and visualization. The life cycle of the spatial database is not as linear as the trapping database but like the trapping database, it has an annual life cycle. Figure 6.4 shows the main elements of the spatial data life cycle. Currently, the trapping and spatial database are separate, and incorporating trapping data into the spatial database requires the use of conversion routines. Future plans call for the development of an integrated database that allows for more flexible use of the trapping data and more efficient data analysis, production, visualization, and delivery.

The STS GIS database holds a complete collection of ancillary data layers for use in analysis and mapping as well as seasonal trapping layers. The predetermined trap layer is used in the generation of cooperator field maps and as a base layer in the project's ArcIMS map server. Cooperator field maps generally are created using georeferenced USGS Digital Raster Graphic images as a map base with the predetermined site locations, target circles, and site list printed on the digital map base (Fig. 6.5). The Information Systems Group at Michigan State University produces more than 1,500 field maps each season in support of trap placement and inspection.

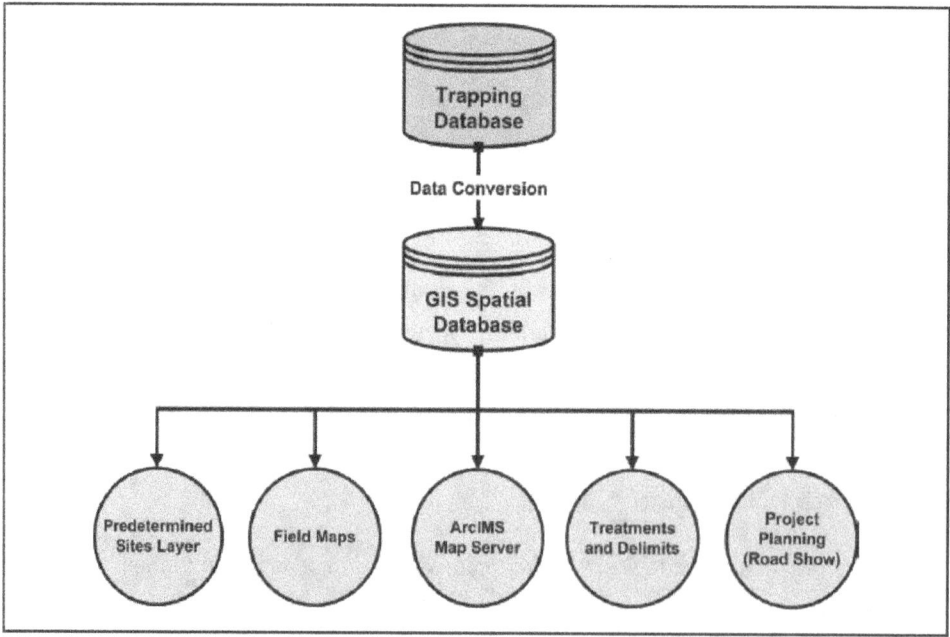

Figure 6.4.—*Main elements of the spatial data life cycle.*

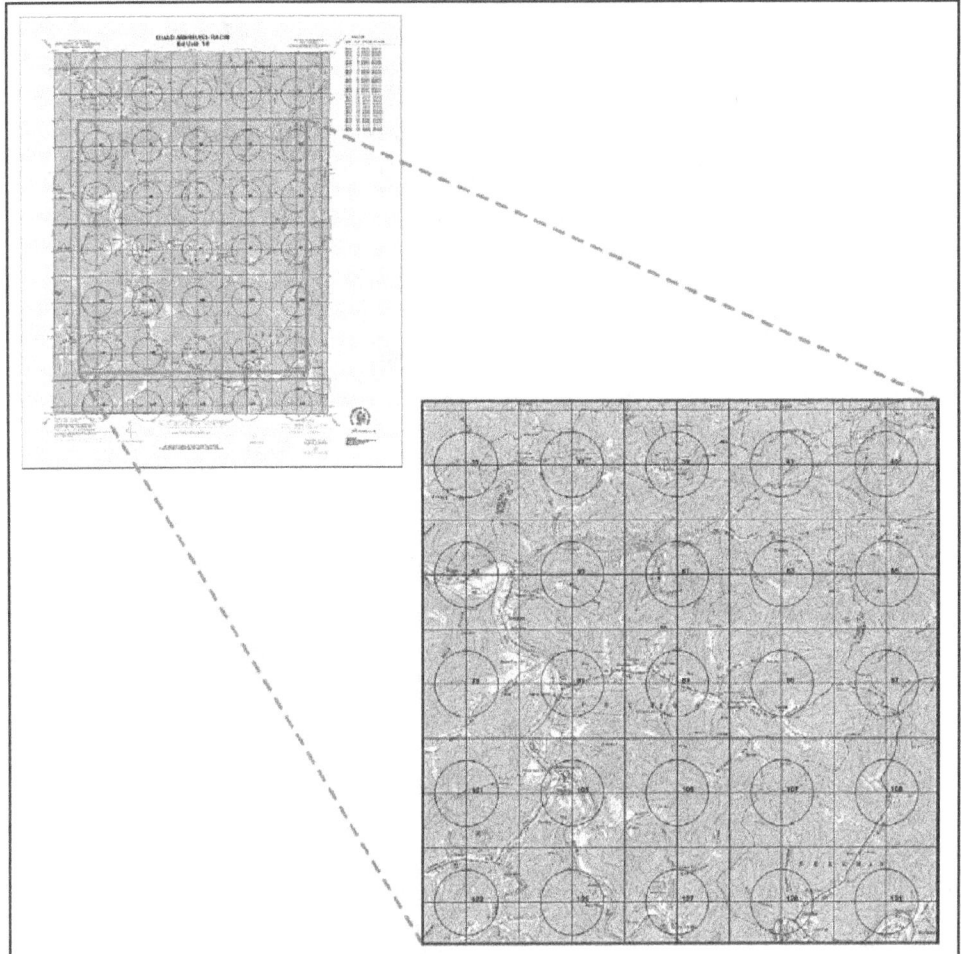

Figure 6.5.—*DRG field map used for the placement of traps.*

Specialized GIS tools are used to delineate, delimit, and create treatment boundaries during and after the project planning meetings (Chapter 7). Initial delimit and treatment boundaries are determined during the annual cooperator planning meetings held between September and November. Cooperators use customized GIS tools developed by members of the STS Information Systems Group for the management of these boundary data layers. Updates are made to the boundaries by cooperators and then transferred to the Information Systems Group at Virginia Tech for insertion into the STS spatial database. New data are added as versioned data layers and GIS technicians process these versioned layers into final published data when all edits have been made by the cooperator. The versioning capabilities of the spatial database give technicians better control over the final data product by allowing them to manage cooperator changes in the form of distinct data layers. This allows changes to the boundaries to be rolled back by the removal of a versioned layer rather than repeatedly editing a single master layer to incorporate cooperator updates.

Information Delivery

Information delivery through the IT infrastructure of STS (Fig. 6.6) is an important integrative component of the operational project. The integrative functions served by the IT infrastructure have been integral to the project's success. Real-time or near real-time delivery of data and derived products allow cooperators to maintain a high degree of data ownership and connectivity to other cooperators.

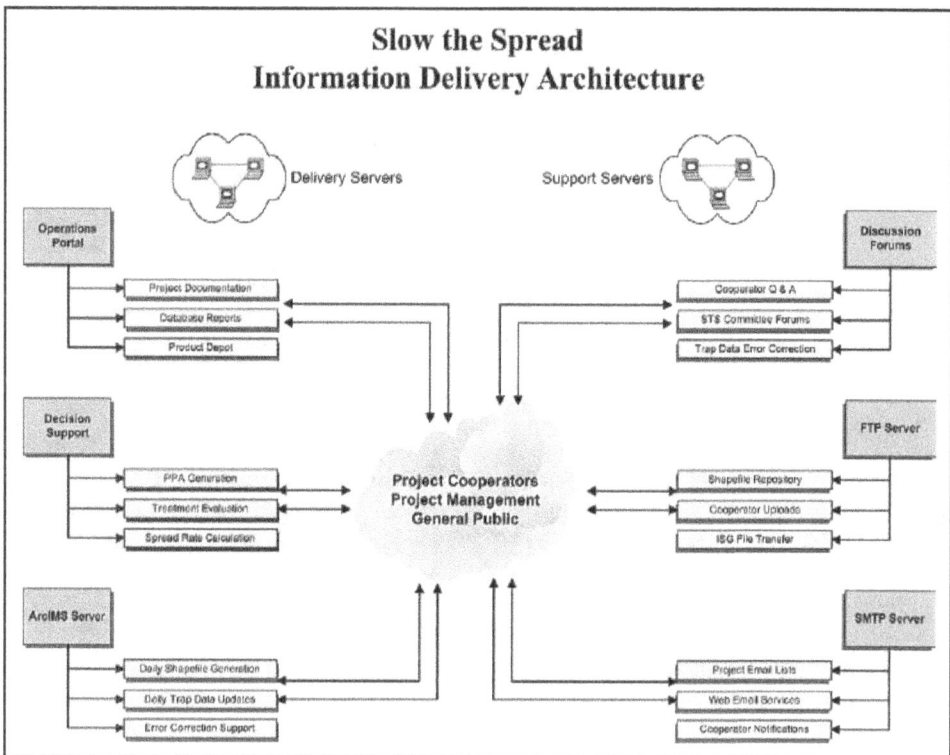

Figure 6.6.—*Resource groups of the STS information delivery architecture.*

Web Servers

The primary information delivery web servers operated by the STS Information Systems Group in support of the STS Program are the *Gypsy Moth Slow the Spread Foundation, Operations Portal, Decision Support System*, and *ArcIMS Map Server* Web sites. The servers can be categorized into two groups: Delivery Servers and Support Servers (Table 6.5). These web servers are the primary vehicle for distributing project documentation, data, software, and products. The project's web sites are served by the Apache HTTPD web server application. Perl and PHP are used to develop dynamic pages and provide web access to the project's distributed database.

Table 6.5.—*Web servers operated by the STS Information Systems Group*

WWW.GMSTS.ORG
The official Internet entry point for the STS Program for cooperators and the general public. This site provides links to the main program operations servers as well as access to administrative and grant-related documents. Cooperators can find minutes of Board of Directors meetings and conference calls, Foundation bylaws, sample member state agreement, annual reports, grant applications, and fiscal reporting guidelines.

OPERATIONS.GMSTS.ORG
The main entry point for cooperators who access the STS Program on a daily basis. Cooperators and Program personnel can access a variety of instructional guidelines and documents related to the trapping protocols defined for the STS Program. Real-time reporting from the trap database is available, as are numerous fact sheets covering an array of technical areas. This also is the main access point for cooperator error correction of trap data. The Product Depot provides customized access to data. Many components are dynamic and rely on information contained in the STS database for the real-time generation of the web page.

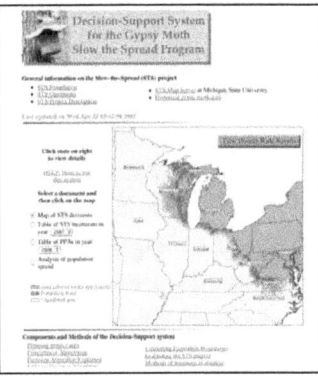

DA.GMSTS.ORG
The Decision Support System site contains the Decision Algorithm and associated derived products. It provides access to current data output by the decision model as well as an historical archive of spread rate analysis and treatment evaluation. Also available are treatment and delimit recommendations based on current trap data retrieved from the distributed trapping database. The data on this site are updated every 24 hours, which is the main integrative resource for the planning process. The site's visualization and GIS analysis modules were developed by STS Program personnel.

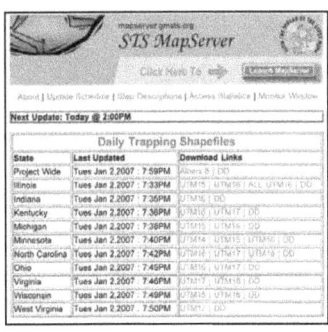

MAPSERVER.GMSTS.ORG
The ESRI ArcIMS map server allows the visualization and querying of trapping data on a near real-time basis. Trap data are extracted from the trapping database three times daily, and the map-server trapping layers are updated with the generated shapefiles. The files are also available for downloading from the map-server monitoring web page available from the operations portal.

Table 6.5.—*Web servers operated by the STS Information Systems Group (continued)*

MAIL.GMSTS.ORG
The program mail server provides e-mail services in the form of distribution lists, support for CGI applications, and e-mail based reports. The distribution lists are updated based on a scripted routine that queries a directory table within the STS database and generates committee e-mail lists based upon associated attributes.

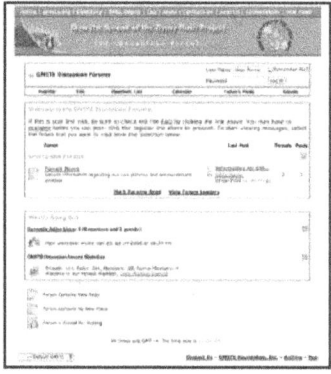

FORUMS.GMSTS.ORG
The STS discussion forums Web site provides a centralized means of communication between and among cooperators and Program support personnel. The discussion forum site has proven useful with respect to correcting errors in trap data. The threaded organizational structure of a discussion forum provides an ease of use which cooperators find more user-friendly than e-mail.

FTP.GMSTS.ORG
Accessible by login for uploading using an FTP client or via the Operations Portal for downloading (www.gmsts.org/ftp), the FTP server is a central file repository for cooperators and Program coordinators.

The IT architecture of the STS Program is a dynamic component of the STS operational infrastructure. The techniques used in delivering information through these Internet resources are constantly being refined to improve the flexibility, speed, and efficiency of delivery. As the design of the project's Internet resources becomes more complex, a design philosophy has evolved that focuses on a development framework consisting of dynamic rather than static components. This is steering future development in the direction of more database-driven backend components.

Summary

In this chapter we described the data management and information delivery framework used by the STS Program. The discussion of the data life cycle was started in Chapter 3, which focused on field data collection, and was continued in this chapter, starting with the submission of data to the project database. This was followed by a review of the remaining elements of the data life cycle, and the integration with the spatial database and project GIS was reviewed. Additional key concepts highlighted in this chapter were 1) the use of a central data management structure; 2) the accessibility of data to cooperators, which fosters a high degree of ownership by cooperators; 3) the automation of data management, which is a key element of data flow success; and 4) the use of the Internet to provide a rapid means of information delivery.

The data management and information delivery infrastructure outlined in Chapters 3 to 5 represents the evolution of a process that began more than 15 years ago for managing an increasingly complex gypsy moth project. The lessons that were learned, having spanned both the pre- and post-Internet boom eras, provide coordinators of the STS Program with a unique perspective on designing, deploying, and managing a wide-area integrated pest management project for invasive species. The final chapter addresses the organizational structure and operational aspects of the STS Program.

Chapter 7. Project Organization, Planning, and Operations

Donna S. Leonard[1]

Introduction

By 1997, results from the 5-year pilot phase of the Slow the Spread (STS) Program had clearly demonstrated that it was biologically, economically, and environmentally feasible to reduce the rate at which the gypsy moth was spreading in the United States. At this point, planning for integration of the STS Program into the USDA's national strategy for managing the gypsy moth became a priority. The transition from pilot to operational status occurred over a 3-year period (1998 to 2000) and resulted in many changes in project structure and organization.

The national STS Program is not only effective but unique in that it incorporates an innovative management structure along with leading edge technology in the arenas of data management and computer-aided decision support. Monitoring conducted under STS and housed in our distributed database is the largest and most complete source of data on the establishment and spread of an invasive species. STS also is the largest user of mating disruption in the world. Efforts to develop and improve the efficient application of mating-disruption tactics began under the Appalachian Integrated Pest Management Demonstration Project, and efforts to refine this technology continue today under STS. Finally, the management structure for implementing STS, the Gypsy Moth Slow the Spread Foundation, Inc., with a representative from each state making up the Board of Directors, is a novel approach to managing invasive forest insect pests.

The structure required to manage the pilot project was relatively simple because the number of partners in the project was fairly small. Oversight was provided by a steering committee consisting of representatives from the Forest Service, USDA Animal Plant Health and Inspection Service (APHIS), and participating states. Expert recommendations on the technical aspects of the project were provided by a technical committee consisting of scientists from the Forest Service, APHIS, states, and universities. Overall coordination was provided by a Forest Service project manager who also chaired the technical committee. During the pilot project, the small number of partners allowed the technical committee to be fully integrated with all project operations. This is not the case with the national program.

[1] USDA Forest Service, Forest Health Protection, P.O. Box 2680, Asheville, North Carolina 28802.

As the project transitioned from pilot to operational status in the late 1990's and the area under management increased from 7 to 50 million acres, so did the number of partners cooperating in STS. The national program includes partners from USDA, 10 states, and 2 universities that provide data management and GIS support (Table 7.1). The sheer number of groups involved in implementing the national program presented unique challenges with respect to designing an appropriate management structure. In this chapter I discuss the rationale that led to the formation of the STS Foundation and summarize the organizational structure used to plan and implement the project.

Table 7.1.—*Key Partners in gypsy moth STS Program as of 2005*

Federal
USDA Animal and Plant Health Inspection Service
USDA Forest Service
State[a]
Illinois Department of Agriculture
Indiana Department of Natural Resources
Office of the State Entomologist, University of Kentucky
Michigan Department of Agriculture
Minnesota Department of Agriculture
North Carolina Department of Agriculture and Consumer Services
Ohio Department of Agriculture
Virginia Department of Agriculture and Consumer Services
West Virginia Department of Agriculture
Wisconsin Department of Agriculture, Trade and Consumer Protection
University
Michigan State University
Virginia Polytechnic Institute and State University

[a] Iowa and Tennessee are likely to join in the near future.

The STS Foundation: an Organizational Structure to Support the National Program

In the fall of 1997, STS Pilot Project personnel provided thorough briefings to the states that had not been a part of the pilot project but would be key partners in a national project. These included Wisconsin, Illinois, Indiana, and Ohio. Once consensus for the project had been reached among all eight states, the Steering Committee from the pilot project was expanded to include the Plant Regulatory Official from each of the new states. This group was tasked with designing a management framework that would support the successful implementation of a national STS Program as well as continued oversight of the ongoing pilot project. The Steering Committee compiled a list of components that it believed were critical to the successful implementation of a wide-area, barrier-zone project such as STS. The following were the initial components:

1. Multiple administrative and jurisdictional units that cooperated in one management structure.
2. Federal resources allocated on the basis of biological need rather than jurisdictional or administrative boundaries.
3. Allocation of federal resources to be based on group discussion and decisions.
4. The ability to pool state resources as cost share on federal grant(s).
5. Use of a central database integrated with GIS, rapid turnaround from field data collection to storage in a database, and the display of information and data on the Internet.
6. Intensive monitoring using pheromone-baited traps deployed in standardized arrays and treatment of detected populations according to program protocols.
7. Use of computer-based algorithms and models for decision support.
8. Mechanisms to contract for services or goods that are needed projectwide.
9. Information, education, and enhanced regulatory activities.

After the list was compiled, the suitability of different management structures to meet these needs was evaluated. The standard Federal method of funding projects through grants to individual states participating in STS was insufficient in meeting many of the listed components. In particular, grants to individual states would not support the critical components 1, 2, 3, 4, and 8. An alternative management structure was designed to meet the specific needs of the project—a nonprofit foundation with each participating state providing a member to the Board of Directors. This structure now unifies the partners, increases the states' ownership of and accountability for the program, promotes planning and implementation based on biological need rather than jurisdictional boundaries, allows the states to pool their resources for the required cost share, and facilitates the uniform implementation of trapping procedures, database management, and treatment decisions.

USDA Organization and Delivery

Since the inception of the pilot project, the USDA Forest Service has been designated as the lead agency for the implementation of STS. The Southern Region's Forest Health Protection unit has provided a program manager for STS since its inception as a pilot project. As the pilot project transitioned to a national program that included additional states from the Forest Service's Northeastern Area, the decision to retain a national program manager in the Southern Region was made in part to support the states' desire for a unified management structure. The Forest Service allocates annual funding of approximately $10 million each year for the trapping, treatment, data management, and technology development aspects of the STS Program.

The Plant Protection and Quarantine (PPQ) program within APHIS also has responsibilities in implementing STS. During the pilot project, PPQ provided seed money for enhanced regulatory activities within the STS action zone. These activities reaped rewards in identifying the sources of introduction and were expanded when the project transitioned from pilot status to a national program. PPQ allocates annual funding of approximately $270,000 each year for this purpose.

The Forest Service and APHIS are not members of the STS Foundation; however, the Forest Service program manager routinely participates in Foundation meetings and conference calls. The program manager is responsible for coordinating the project, reporting accomplishments on a national level, recommending budget allocations to the partners, formulating the national work plan, and chairing the Operations Committee.

Planning in the National STS Program

Each year, the STS Foundation Board of Directors formulates a projectwide budget and plan of work based on recommendations from the Operations Committee, the Technical Committee, and the USDA. Survey costs are fairly stable from year to year and across state boundaries, and total acreage recommended for treatment by the STS decision-support system also is somewhat predictable. However, the locations of the treatments are highly variable from year to year. This would make state planning and budgeting to meet cost share difficult under a traditional management structure with individual grants to each state. Under the Foundation management structure, Federal funds needed to implement the project are passed to the Foundation in a single grant. State members pool their resources to meet cost share and Federal funds are allocated to each state through subgrants according to biological need rather than ability to meet cost share. In this manner, the STS Foundation can ensure that all actions necessary to meet project goals are implemented each year. The Foundation's organizational structure is shown in Figure 7.1.

Board of Directors, STS Foundation

The Board of Directors consists of the State Plant Regulatory Official from 8 of the 10 states that are partners in STS. Ohio and Kentucky are not formally represented on the board but they receive funding through the Foundation and participate in board and other committee meetings. The board conducts an annual meeting in February. At this time, the STS Program Manager presents to the board the accomplishment report for the preceding year, the plan of work for the coming year as drafted by the Operations Committee, and a draft budget. A unified budget that includes both Federal and state resources is approved by the board and timelines for submitting grant packages are also

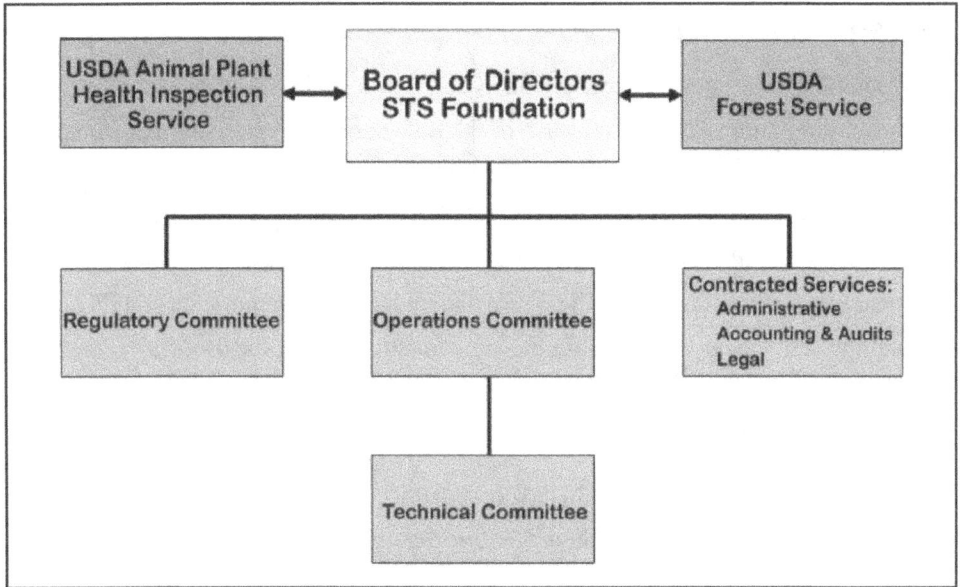

Figure 7.1.—*Organizational structure of the STS Foundation.*

outlined at this meeting. During the remainder of the year, the board uses monthly conference calls to review grant compliance and the status of projects, and address other issues that might arise. Benchmarks in the creation and operation of the STS Foundation are listed in Table 7.2.

Table 7.2.—*Benchmarks in the formation and operations of STS Foundation*

1998	Steering Committee votes to use a nonprofit STS Foundation as official management structure for the implementation of STS Program. Bylaws and state member agreements drafted. A firm of attorneys is hired as legal counsel.
1999	STS Foundation incorporated in Raleigh, North Carolina. The Commissioners of Agriculture North Carolina, Virginia, West Virginia, Indiana, Illinois, Wisconsin and Michigan sign member agreements appointing the Plant Regulatory Official from each state as a member on the Foundation's Board of Directors. Ohio's participation in STS was critical, but Ohio law prevents State officials from joining corporate boards, including those of nonprofit corporations. Ohio elects to participate in STS without signing formal agreement or appointing a member to Foundation Board.
2000	Appropriations bill for FY 2000 includes earmark to "fully fund the gypsy moth Slow the Spread Program." USDA Forest Service allocates $8 million toward the Program; cost share set to ensure Forest Service expenditures do not exceed 75 percent of the total cost to implement Program.
	Higher than normal Federal cost share (75 vs. 50 percent) deemed necessary for national STS Program because all costs would be absorbed by states in implementation area while states (south or west) outside of implementation area would receive bulk of Program benefits. The first Board of Directors meeting held in November 2000.
2001	Kentucky joins STS Program.
2002	Forest Service increases allocation to $10 million following recommendation that large areas on National Forests within Program area be treated.
2004	Minnesota joins STS Program.

Operations Committee

The Operations Committee, chaired by the Forest Service STS Program Manager, consists of program managers from each of the state partners, representatives from the data management groups at Virginia Tech and Michigan State University, the chair of the Technical Committee, and other Forest Service staff. The Operations Committee meets in January and August each year. The winter meeting focuses on finalizing treatment recommendations, trapping plans, and budgets. The summer meeting focuses on data flow and the development of new tools for streamlining the process.

Technical Committee

The Technical Committee, chaired by a Forest Service research scientist, is composed of various technical experts from the USDA, universities, and other state agencies. The committee meets once a year and has responsibility for: 1) reviewing the operational plans relative to compliance with existing project standards and protocols; 2) identifying problem areas where the standards and protocols are not working or are not followed; and 3) identifying, prioritizing, planning, and budgeting for technology development projects needed to address problems. The chair of the Technical Committee also is on the Operations Committee and provides regular updates and moderates discussions between the two committees to facilitate technical needs and updates of STS. There also are members at the Federal, state, and university levels that are active on both committees. The chair of the Technical Committee also interacts directly with the STS Foundation Board of Directors.

Regulatory Committee

The Regulatory Committee, co-chaired by APHIS and a state partner, is composed of representatives from each group that receives APHIS funds to implement the regulatory component of STS. This group typically meets once a year in conjunction with the Operations Committee's January meeting.

Data Flow, Planning, and Decision Making

Data flow (see Fig. 3.6) is described briefly here. During the winter, predetermined trapping grid points are generated at the database and provided to the cooperators for implementation the following summer. Trapping data are collected using handheld GPS units; the GPS files are downloaded to a laptop computer in the field each week and then uploaded to the database using tools that check for common formatting errors. Once in the database, the GPS files are validated: "good" data go into the database and "bad" data are posted back to cooperators for on-line correction. Immediately after data being posted to the database, the data are available to cooperators in several formats: tabular reports, preformatted maps at the decision-support Web site, shapefiles for use in ArcGIS, or interactive maps on the mapserver.

Final trapping data are analyzed by the STS Decision Algorithm (Chapters 4 and 5), which streamlines planning and helps ensure that standardized decision processes are used across jurisdictional and administrative boundaries. The Decision Algorithm uses moth capture data to measure the year-to-year spread of the gypsy moth, establish project boundaries, detect potential problem areas (PPAs) where the data suggest new gypsy moth infestations, prioritize and recommend action for each PPA, and evaluate treatments.

Once moth capture data are finalized in the late summer and early fall, output from the Decision Algorithm is used to formulate a plan of work for each state and then for the entire project. This is done in a series of meetings between the Forest Service program manager and the individual states. The items that define the project structure for the coming year (project boundaries, trapping arrays, and treatment blocks) are captured in an ArcGIS project and posted to the database and the decision-support web pages. Plans are revised based on public input during environmental analyses and available funding. The final draft of the project-wide plan of work is revised by the Operations Committee at its January meeting and forwarded to the Board of Directors for review and approval at its annual meeting in February. Once the work plan and budget are approved, the database starts the entire cycle over again by distributing predetermined trapping grid points to the cooperators for implementation.

Implementation of STS on Mixed Land Ownership

The STS Program is a barrier-zone program designed to minimize the spread of the gypsy moth. As with any barrier-zone program, STS is only as strong as its weakest link; that is, it is critically important that all land owners and managers within the STS Program area support its success and implement the program uniformly across the entire band. This has been challenging because the 50-million-acre band where intensive survey and treatment activities are implemented is a mosaic of private, local, state, Federal, and tribal-owned or managed lands. Also, the policies, goals, and objectives on these parcels are as varied as the ownership patterns. For example, on the Federal side alone there are more than 50 facilities that fall within the STS area. This currently includes 7 National Forests, 8 wilderness areas, 12 military bases, more than a dozen recreation lakes managed by the U.S. Army Corps of Engineers, 9 USDI Fish and Wildlife Refuges, a dozen National Parks and Monuments, and 2 Department of Energy facilities.

To ensure that the STS trapping and treatment protocols are understood and followed once a new state becomes a formal STS partner, Program personnel work with them prior to arrival of gypsy moth in that state. For example, STS Program staff began coordinating with Minnesota personnel several years before the STS area actually entered that State. Seed money and GPS units were provided and personnel from the STS Information Systems Group worked with State personnel to convert their trapping program to metric spacing and to coordinate collection and submission of their trap data per STS protocols. In this manner, the transition to a new set of trapping and treatment protocols was complete by the time Minnesota became a formal member of the STS Foundation and began to implement the project on state and private lands under its authority.

However, on Federally owned land, this issue can be slightly more complex due to the number of Federal facilities that fall within or just in advance of the STS Program area. Under the pilot project when there were only a handful of federal facilities, STS Program funding was provided directly to each facility who then conducted the trapping on Federal lands. However, trapping protocols were not always maintained in a uniform manner as is required under STS. To maintain uniformity across administrative boundaries in the manner originally intended, STS has adopted a revised strategy based on the lessons learned under the pilot project.

For trapping on Federally owned land, STS Program personnel meet with managers who have oversight of the Federal facility to brief them on the STS Program and its goals. Permission is then requested for state employees to deploy traps on the Federal land. Upon receiving permission, trapping is conducted by the STS state partner and is incorporated into the trapping plan for the entire state and funded through the STS Foundation. In this manner, trapping standards are maintained.

Although STS shares all data with these Federal facilities, the data are managed by the STS Program. If the trap-catch data suggest that a treatment is needed for a new gypsy moth population, the Federal manager is again briefed, treatment options are presented, and the planning required for treatment is initiated and funded. Contracting for aerial application services on federal land also is done by STS Program personnel to simplify treatment deployments at the state level. This process ensures that STS standards are met and remain uniform throughout the entire project area, and minimizes the time and resources that a Federal facility must invest to cooperate in the STS program, thus ensuring its participation.

Afterword

The success of any area-wide integrated pest management program depends heavily on the ability of cooperators at the Federal and state level to transcend geopolitical boundaries in pursuit of a common goal. The Slow the Spread Program is a quintessential example of how a universal regional strategy for managing a nonindigenous species, such as the gypsy moth, can be implemented while still allowing those at the state level to coordinate their own activities within a common framework.

This General Technical Report first detailed the history of the gypsy moth in North America, followed by a discussion of the dynamics of its spread. Quantitative approaches to understanding the gypsy moth invasion in North America have been a particularly successful application of mathematical ecology in support of an effective management strategy such as STS. The remaining chapters traced the path of the STS philosophy and implementation, including data collection, analysis and interpretation, and project planning and evaluation. The development and use of geospatial technologies in the STS Program have occurred in parallel with the development of web-based resources, an integral component to this regional program.

Results to date indicate that most treatments deployed under the STS Program have been successful and that the overall objective, a 50-percent reduction in annual rates of gypsy moth spread, has been exceeded. It is noteworthy that this is being accomplished in a program in which about half of the resources are allocated to monitoring, and that treatments are applied on only about 1 percent of the acreage in the management area. It also is noteworthy that tactics specific to the gypsy moth are deployed on more than 70 percent of the area that is treated. The success of the STS Program demonstrates the benefit of area-wide integrated pest management on a variety of landscapes, and the program could serve as a conceptual framework upon which to base other management programs that target nonindigenous invaders.

Literature Cited

Abbott, W.S. 1925. **A method of computing the effectiveness of an insecticide.** Journal of Economic Entomology. 18: 265-267.

Allee, W.C. 1932. **Animal aggregations: a study in general sociology.** Chicago, IL: University of Chicago Press.

Andow, D.A.; Kareiva, P.M.; Levin, S.A.; Okubo, A. 1990. **Spread of invading organisms.** Landscape Ecology. 4: 177-188.

Beirne, B. 1975. **Biological control attempts by introductions against pest insects in the field in Canada.** Canadian Entomologist. 107: 225-236.

Beroza, M.; Knipling, E.F. 1972. **Gypsy moth control with the sex attractant pheromone.** Science. 177: 19-27.

Bierl, B.A.; Beroza, M.; Collier, C.W. 1970. **Potent sex attractant of the gypsy moth: its isolation, identification and synthesis.** Science. 170: 87-89.

Blacksten, R.; Herzer, I.; and Kessler, C. 1978. **A cost/benefit analysis for gypsy moth containment.** Rep. KFR 161-78. Arlington, VA: U.S. Department of Agriculture.

Burgess, A.F. 1930. **The gipsy moth and the brown-tail moth.** Farm. Bull. 1623. Washington, DC: U.S. Department of Agriculture.

Campbell, R.W.; Sloan, R.J. 1977. **Natural regulation of innocuous gypsy moth populations.** Environmental Entomology. 6: 315-322.

Clark, J.S.; Lewis, M.A.; Horvath, L. 2001. **Invasion by extremes: population spread with variation in dispersal and reproduction.** American Naturalist. 157: 537-554.

Courchamp, F.; Clutton-Brock, T.; Grenfell, B. 1999. **Inverse density dependence and the Allee effect.** Trends in Ecology and Evolution. 14: 405-410.

Davidson, C.B.; Gottschalk, K.W.; Johnson, J.E. 2001. **European gypsy moth (*Lymantria dispar* L.) outbreaks: a review of the literature.** Gen. Tech. Rep. NE-278. Newtown Square, PA: U.S. Department of Agriculture, Forest Service, Northeastern Research Station. 15 p.

Deutsch, C.V.; Journel, A.G. 1992. **GSLIB. Geostatistical software library and user's guide.** Oxford, UK: Oxford University Press.

Doane, C.C.; McManus, M.L.,eds. 1981. **The gypsy moth: research toward integrated pest management.** Tech. Bull. 1584. Washington, DC: U.S. Department of Agriculture.

Dobson, A.P.; May, R.M. 1986. **Patterns of invasions by pathogens and parasites.** In: Mooney, H.A.; Drake, J.A., eds. Ecology of biological invasions of North America and Hawaii. New York: Springer-Verlag.

Drake, J.M. 2004. **Allee effects and the risk of biological invasion.** Risk Analysis. 24: 795-802.

Dunlap, T.R. 1980. **The gypsy moth: a study in science and public policy.** Journal of Forest History. 24: 116-126.

Elkinton, J.S.; Carde, R.T. 1980. **Distribution, dispersal, and apparent survival of male gypsy moths *Lymantria dispar* as determined by capture in pheromone-baited traps.** Environmental Entomology. 9: 729-737.

Elkinton, J.S.; Liebhold, A.M. 1990. **Population dynamics of gypsy moth in North America.** Annual Review of Entomology. 35: 571-596.

Elkinton, J.S.; Liebhold, A.M.; Muzika, R.M. 2004. **Effects of alternative prey on predation by small mammals on gypsy moth pupae.** Population Ecology. 46: 171-178.

Elkinton, J.S.; Healy, W.M.; Buonaccorsi, J.P.; Boettner, G.H.; Hazzard, A.M.; Smith, H.R.; Liebhold, A.M. 1996. **Interactions among gypsy moths, white-footed mice, and acorns.** Ecology. 77: 2332-2342.

Fagan, W.F.; Lewis, M.A.; Neubert, M.G.; van den Driessche, P. 2002. **Invasion theory and biological control.** Ecology Letters. 5: 148-157.

Felt, E.P. 1942. **The gypsy moth threat in the United States.** Eastern Plant Board Circ. No.1.

Fisher, R.A. 1937. **The wave of advance of advantageous genes.** Annals of Eugenics. 7: 255-369.

Fleischer, S.; Roberts, A.; Young, J.; Mahoney, P.; Ravlin, F.W.; Reardon, R. 1992. **Development of geographic information system technology for gypsy moth management within a county: an overview.** NA-TP-01-93. Radnor, PA: U.S. Department of Agriculture, Forest Service, Northeastern Area, State and Private Forestry.

Forbush, E.H.; Fernald, C.H. 1896. **The gypsy moth.** Boston, MA: Wright and Potter Printing Co.

Gypsy Moth Digest. 2005. **Gypsy moth defoliation.** Morgantown, WV: U.S. Department of Agriculture, Forest Service, Northeastern Area, State and Private Forestry. Available at http://na.fs.fed.us/wv/gmdigest/index.html.

Hengeveld, R. 1989. **Dynamics of biological invasions.** London: Chapman and Hall.

Howard, L.O. 1930. **A history of applied entomology.** Misc. Collect. 84. Washington, DC: Smithsonian Institution.

Isaaks, E.H.; Srivastava, R.M. 1989. **An introduction to applied geostatistics.** New York: Oxford University Press.

Iwaki, S.; Marumo, S.; Saito, T.; Yamada, M.; Katagiri, K. 1974. **Synthesis and activity of optically active disparlure.** Journal of the American Chemical Society. 96: 7842-7844.

Johnson, D.M.; Liebhold, A.M.; Tobin, P.C.; Bjørnstad, O.N. 2006. **Allee effects and pulsed invasion by the gypsy moth.** Nature. 444: 361-363.

Kean, J.M.; Barlow, N.D. 2000. **Effects of dispersal on local population increase.** Ecology Letters. 3: 479-482.

Leonard, D.S.; Sharov, A.A. 1995. **Slow the Spread Project update: developing a process for evaluation.** In: Fosbroke, S.L.C.; Gottschalk, K.W., eds. Proceedings: USDA interagency gypsy moth research forum; 1995 January 17-20; Annapolis, MD. Gen. Tech. Rep. NE-213. Radnor, PA: U.S. Department of Agriculture, Forest Service, Northeastern Forest Experiment Station: 82-85.

Leonhardt, B.A.; Mastro, V.C.; Leonard, D.S.; McLane, W.; Reardon, R.C.; Thorpe, K.W. 1996. **Control of low-density gypsy moth (Lepidoptera: Lymantriidae) populations by mating disruption with pheromone.** Journal of Chemical Ecology. 22: 1255-1272.

Leung, B.; Drake, J.A.; Lodge, D.M. 2004. **Predicting invasions: propagule pressure and the gravity of Allee effects.** Ecology. 85: 1651-1660.

Leuschner, W.A. 1991. **Gypsy moth containment program economic assessment. Final Report.** Blacksburg, VA: Virginia Polytechnic Institute and State University, Department of Forestry.

Leuschner, W.A.; Young, J.A.; Waldon, S.A.; Ravlin, F.W. 1996. **Potential benefits of slowing the gypsy moth's spread.** Southern Journal of Applied Forestry. 20: 65-73.

Lewis, M.A.; Kareiva, P. 1993. **Allee dynamics and the spread of invading organisms.**

Theoretical Population Biology. 43: 141-158.

Liebhold, A.M.; Bascompte, J. 2003. **The Allee effect, stochastic dynamics and the eradication of alien species.** Ecology Letters. 6: 133-140.

Liebhold, A.M.; Tobin, P.C. 2006. **Growth of newly established alien populations: comparison of North American gypsy moth colonies with invasion theory.** Population Ecology. 48: 253-262.

Liebhold, A.M.; Halverson, J.A.; Elmes, G.A. 1992. **Gypsy moth invasion in North America: a quantitative analysis.** Journal of Biogeography. 19: 513-520.

Liebhold, A.M.; Mastro, V.; Schaefer, P.W. 1989. **Learning from the legacy of Léopold Trouvelot.** Bulletin of the Entomological Society of America. 35: 20-22.

Liebhold, A.M.; MacDonald, W.L.; Bergdahl, D.D.; Mastro, V. 1995. **Invasion by exotic forest pests: a threat to forest ecosystems.** Forest Science Monographs. 30: 1-49.

Liebhold, A.; Thorpe, K.; Ghent, J.; Lyons, D.B. 1994. **Gypsy moth egg mass sampling for decision-making: a users' guide.** NA-TP-04-94. Radnor, PA: U.S. Department of Agriculture, Forest Service, Northeastern Area, State and Private Forestry.

Liebhold, A.; Luzader, E.; Reardon, R.; Bullard, A.; Roberts, A.; Ravlin, W.; DeLost, S.; Spears, B. 1996. **Use of a geographical information system to evaluate regional treatment effects in a gypsy moth (Lepidoptera: Lymantriidae) management program.** Journal of Economic Entomology. 17: 560-566.

MacArthur, R.H.; Wilson, E.O. 1967. **The theory of island biogeography.** Princeton, NJ: Princeton University Press.

Madrid, F.J.; Stewart, R.K. 1981. **The influence of some environmental factors on the development and behavior of the gypsy moth (*Lymantria dispar* L.) in Quebec.** Annals of the Entomological Society of Quebec. 26: 191-211.

Mason, C.J.; McManus, M.L. 1981. **Larval dispersal of the gypsy moth.** In: Doane, C.C.; McManus, M.L., eds. The gypsy moth: research toward integrated pest management. Tech. Bull. 1584. Washington, DC: U.S. Department of Agriculture: 161-202.

McFadden, M.W.; McManus, M.E. 1991. **An insect out of control? The potential for spread and establishment of the gypsy moth in new forest areas in the United States.** In: Baranchikov, Y.N.; Mattson, W.J.; Hain, F.P.; Payne, T.L., eds. Forest insect guilds: patterns of interaction with host trees. Gen. Tech. Rep. NE-153. Radnor, PA: U.S. Department of Agriculture, Forest Service, Northeastern Forest Experiment Station: 172-186.

McManus, M.L. 1978. **Expanded gypsy moth research and development program.** Journal of Forestry. 76: 144-149.

Mollison, D.; Anderson, R.M.; Bartlett, M.S.; Southwood, R. 1986. **Modeling biological invasions: chance, explanation, prediction.** Ser. B: Philosophical Transactions of the Royal Society of London. Biological Sciences. 314: 675-693.

Mori, K.; Takigawa, T.; Matsui, M. 1976. **Stereoselective synthesis of optically active disparlure, the pheromone of the gypsy moth (*Porthetria dispar* L.).** Tetrahedron Letters. 44: 3953-3956.

Morin, R.S.; Liebhold, A.M.; Luzader, E.R.; Lister, A.J.; Gottschalk, K.W.; Twardus, D.B. 2004. **Mapping host-species abundance of three major exotic forest pests.** Res. Pap. NE-726. Newtown Square, PA: U.S. Department of Agriculture, Forest Service, Northeastern Research Station. 11 p.

Myers, J.H.; Simberloff, D.S.; Kuris, A.M.; Carey, J.R. 2000. **Eradication revisited: dealing with exotic species.** Trends in Ecology and Evolution. 15: 316-320.

National Research Council. 2002. **Predicting invasions of nonindigenous plants and plant pests.** Washington, DC: National Academy Press.

Perry, C.C. 1955. **Gypsy moth appraisal program and proposed plan to prevent spread of the moths.** Tech. Bull. 1124. Washington, DC: U.S. Department of Agriculture.

Ravlin, F.W. 1991. **Development of monitoring and decision-support systems for integrated pest management of forest defoliators in North America.** Forest Ecology and Management. 39: 3-13.

Ravlin, F.W.; Bellinger, R.G.; Roberts, E.A. 1987. **Status of gypsy moth management programs in the United States: status, evaluation, and recommendations.** Bulletin of the Entomological Society of America. 33: 90-98.

Ravlin, F.W.; Wolfe, R.; Swain, K. 1992. **A strategy to evaluate technologies to slow the spread of the gypsy moth.** Blacksburg, VA: Virginia Polytechnic Institute and State University, Department of Entomology.

Ravlin, F.W.; Fleischer, S.J.; Carter, M.R.; Roberts, E.A.; McManus, M.L. 1991. **A monitoring system for gypsy moth management.** In: Gottschalk, K.W.; Twery, M.J.; Smith, S.I., eds. Proceedings: USDA interagency gypsy moth research forum 1990; East Windsor, CT. Gen. Tech. Rep. NE-146. Radnor, PA: U.S. Department of Agriculture, Forest Service, Northeastern Forest Experiment Station: 89-97.

Reardon, R. 1991. **Appalachian gypsy moth integrated pest management project.** Forest Ecology and Management. 39: 107-112.

Reardon, R. 1996. **Appalachian integrated pest management gypsy moth project: summary and bibliography.** NA-TP-05-96. Radnor, PA: U.S. Department of Agriculture, Forest Service, Northeastern Area, State and Private Forestry.

Reardon, R.; Dubois, N.; McLane, W. 1994. *Bacillus thuringiensis* **for managing gypsy moth: a review.** FHM-NC-01-94. Radnor, PA: U.S. Department of Agriculture, Forest Service, National Center of Forest Health Management.

Reardon, R.C.; Podgwaite, J.; Zerillo, R. 1996. **Gypchek—the gypsy moth nucleopolyhedrosis virus product.** FHTET-96-16. Radnor, PA: U.S. Department of Agriculture, Forest Service, Forest Health Technology Enterprise Team.

Reardon, R.; Venables, L.; Roberts, A. 1993. **The Maryland integrated pest management gypsy moth project 1983-1987.** NA-TP-07-93. Radnor, PA: U.S. Department of Agriculture, Forest Service, Northeastern Area, State and Private Forestry.

Reardon, R.C.; Leonard, D.S.; Mastro, V.C.; Leonhardt, B.A.; McLane, W.; Talley, S.; Thorpe, K.W.; Webb, R.E. 1998. **Using mating disruption to manage gypsy moth: a review.** FHTET-98-01. Radnor, PA: U.S. Department of Agriculture, Forest Service, Forest Health Technology Enterprise Team.

Reardon, R.; McManus, M.L.; Kolodny-Hirsch, D.; Tichenor, R.; Raupp, M.; Schwalbe, C.; Webb, R.; Meckley, P. 1987. **Development and implementation of a gypsy moth integrated pest management program.** Journal of Arboriculture. 13: 209-216.

Régnière, J.; Sharov, A.A. 1998. **Phenology of** *Lymantria dispar* **(Lepidoptera: Lymantriidae) male flight and the effect of moth dispersal in heterogeneous landscapes.** International Journal of Biometeorology. 41: 161-168.

Riis, J.A. 1890. **How the other half lives.** New York: Charles Scribner's Sons.

Riley, C.V.; Vasey, G. 1870. **Imported insects and native American insects.** American Entomologist. 2: 110-112.

Roberts, E.A.; Ravlin, F.W.; Fleischer, S.J. 1993. **Spatial data representation of integrated pest management programs.** American Entomologist. 39: 92-107.

Schwalbe, C.P. 1981. **Disparlure-baited traps for survey and detection.** In: Doane, C.C.; McManus, M.L., eds. The gypsy moth: research toward integrated pest management. Tech. Bull. 1584. Washington, DC: U.S. Department of Agriculture: 542-548.

Sharov, A.A.; Liebhold, A.M. 1998a. **Model of slowing the spread of gypsy moth (Lepidoptera: Lymantriidae) with a barrier zone.** Ecological Applications. 8: 1170-1179.

Sharov, A.A.; Liebhold, A.M. 1998b. **Bioeconomics of managing the spread of exotic pest species with barrier zones.** Ecological Applications. 8: 833-845.

Sharov, A.A.; Liebhold, A.M.; Ravlin, F.W. 1995a. **Prediction of gypsy moth (Lepidoptera: Lymantriidae) mating success from pheromone-baited trap counts.** Environmental Entomology. 24: 1239-1244.

Sharov, A.A.; Liebhold, A.M.; Roberts, E.A. 1997a. **Correlation of counts of gypsy moths (Lepidoptera: Lymantriidae) in pheromone-baited traps with landscape characteristics.** Forest Science. 43: 483-490.

Sharov, A.A.; Liebhold, A.M.; Roberts, E.A. 1997b. **Methods for monitoring the spread of gypsy moth (Lepidoptera: Lymantriidae) populations in the Appalachian mountains.** Journal of Economic Entomology. 90: 1259-1266.

Sharov, A.A.; Liebhold, A.M.; Roberts, E.A. 1998. **Optimizing the use of barrier zones to slow the spread of gypsy moth (Lepidoptera: Lymantriidae) in North America.** Journal of Economic Entomology. 91: 165-174.

Sharov, A.A.; Liebhold, A.M.; Roberts, E.A. 1996a. **Spatial variation among counts of gypsy moths (Lepidoptera: Lymantriidae) in pheromone-baited traps at expanding population fronts.** Environmental Entomology. 25: 1312-1320.

Sharov, A.A.; Liebhold, A.M.; Roberts, E.A. 1996b. **Spread of gypsy moth (Lepidoptera: Lymantriidae) in the central Appalachians: comparison of population boundaries obtained from male moth capture, egg mass counts, and defoliation records.** Environmental Entomology. 25: 783-792.

Sharov, A.A.; Leonard, D.S.; Liebhold, A.M.; Clemens, N.S. 2002a. **Evaluation of preventive treatments in low-density gypsy moth populations.** Journal of Economic Entomology. 95: 1205-1215.

Sharov, A.A.; Pijanowski, B.C.; Liebhold, A.M.; Gage, S.H. 1999. **What affects the rate of gypsy moth (Lepidoptera: Lymantriidae) spread: winter temperature or forest susceptibility.** Agricultural and Forest Entomology. 1: 37-45.

Sharov, A.A.; Roberts, E.A.; Liebhold, A.M.; Ravlin, F.W. 1995b. **Gypsy moth (Lepidoptera: Lymantriidae) spread in the central Appalachians: three methods for species boundary estimation.** Environmental Entomology. 24: 1529-1538.

Sharov, A.A.; Leonard, D.S.; Liebhold, A.M.; Roberts, E.A.; Dickerson, W. 2002b. **Slow the Spread: a national program to contain the gypsy moth.** Journal of Forestry. 100: 30-35.

Sheehan, K.A. 1992. **User's guide for GMPHEN: gypsy moth phenology model.** Gen. Tech. Rep. NE-158. Radnor, PA: U.S. Department of Agriculture, Forest Service, Northeastern Forest Experiment Station. 29 p.

Shigesada, N.; Kawasaki, K. 1997. **Biological invasions: theory and practice.** New York: Oxford University Press.

Shigesada, N.; Kawasaki, K.; Takeda, Y. 1995. **Modeling stratified diffusion in biological invasions.** American Naturalist. 146: 229-251.

Skellam, J.G. 1951. **Random dispersal in theoretical populations.** Biometrika. 38: 196-218.

Stephens, P.A.; Sutherland, W.J. 1999. **Consequences of the Allee effect for behaviour, ecology and conservation.** Trends in Ecology and Evolution. 14: 401-405.

Tcheslavskaia, K.; Brewster, C.C.; Sharov, A.A. 2002. **Mating success of gypsy moth (Lepidoptera: Lymantriidae) females in Southern Wisconsin.** Great Lakes Entomologist. 35: 1-7.

Tobin, P.C.; Liebhold, A.M.; Roberts, E.A. 2007a. **Comparison of methods for estimating the spread of a nonindigenous species.** Journal of Biogeography. 34: 305-312.

Tobin, P.C.; Whitmire, S.L.; Johnson, D.M.; Bjørnstad, O.N.; Liebhold, A.M. 2007b. **Invasion speed is affected by geographic variation in the strength of Allee effects.** Ecology Letters. 10: 36-43.

Tobin, P.C.; Sharov, A.A.; Liebhold, A.M.; Leonard, D.S.; Roberts, E.A.; Learn, M.R. 2004. **Management of the gypsy moth through a decision algorithm under the STS project.** American Entomologist. 50: 200-209.

U.S. Department of Agriculture. 1995. **Gypsy moth management in the United States: a cooperative approach.** Final environmental impact statement. Volumes 1-5. Washington, DC: U.S. Department of Agriculture.

Veit, R.R.; Lewis, M.A. 1996. **Dispersal, population growth, and the Allee effect: dynamics of the house finch invasion of eastern North America.** American Naturalist. 148: 255-274.

Weber, G.A. 1930. **The plant quarantine and control administration: its history, activities and organization.** Washington, DC: Brookings Institute.

Weinberger, H.F.; Lewis, M.A.; Li, B. 2002. **Analysis of linear determinacy for spread in cooperative models.** Journal of Mathematical Biology. 45: 183-218.

Whitmire, S.L.; Tobin, P.C. 2006. **Persistence of invading gypsy moth populations in the United States.** Oecologia. 147: 230-237.

Tobin, Patrick C.; Blackburn, Laura M., eds. 2007. **Slow the Spread: a national program to manage the gypsy moth.** Gen. Tech. Rep. NRS-6. Newtown Square, PA: U.S. Department of Agriculture, Forest Service, Northern Research Station. 109 p.

The gypsy moth is a destructive, nonindigenous pest of forest, shade, and fruit trees that was introduced into the United States in 1869, and is currently established throughout the Northeast and upper Midwest. The Slow the Spread Program is a regional integrated pest management strategy that aims to minimize the rate of gypsy moth spread into uninfested areas. The premise of the Slow the Spread Program is to deploy extensive grids of pheromone-baited traps (>100,000 traps per year) along the expanding population front to identify and subsequently eradicate newly establishing populations to prevent them from growing, coalescing, and contributing to the progression of the population front. This report provides a brief history of the gypsy moth in North America, describes the dynamics of gypsy moth spread, and then details the technological and operational aspects of implementing the Slow the Spread Program.

Key Words: *Lymantria dispar*, biological invasions, integrated pest management, nonindigenous species.